Who Walk Alone

Who Walk Alone

A Consideration of the Single Life

by

MARGARET EVENING

HODDER AND STOUGHTON
LONDON SYDNEY AUCKLAND TORONTO

To the memory of

REV. GWENYTH HUBBLE

Acknowledgments

I<small>T IS WITH A DEEP SENSE OF GRATITUDE THAT I ACKNOWLEDGE</small>
my debt to many friends, both single and married, who have
shared with me their experiences of life—their joy and sadness,
frustration and defeat, freedom and bondage, hopes and
achievements; who have provided me with an abundance of
food for thought out of which this book has emerged slowly and
sometimes painfully. These friends are too numerous to mention
individually, but my grateful thanks to them are none the less
profound and sincere. Some, however, have helped in special
ways during the actual period of writing, by discussion,
commenting on the manuscripts, offering valuable advice and,
in places, causing me to rethink or modify my views. These I
would like specially to mention.

At the outset my most forthright yet kindly critic was my
former Principal, the Rev. Gwenyth Hubble of Toronto. When
I first discussed the outline of the book with her, she gave me
enormous encouragement to go ahead with what seemed an
impossibly daunting task and with typical generosity, offered to
share with me as much as she could of the wisdom and insights
that she had accumulated over many years of counselling
single men and women, particularly missionary candidates
and missionaries on furlough. As students we loved and ad-
mired her for her honesty, clear thinking, rare spiritual insight
and complete lack of 'humbug'—all of which qualities I found
in her comments and criticisms on what I had written. It is a

book which she told me she had 'written many times—in her mind'. Though she never got it down on paper herself, I sometimes felt that she was pouring out much of it to me, and I hope now through me, as we discussed various chapters and as she dipped into her memory bringing out many illustrations and suggestions. I might add that our meetings for discussion were not only extraordinarily helpful and enriching but occasions of much laughter. She had a superb sense of fun!

It was a severe personal blow, therefore, that she died when we were only halfway through what I was fondly coming to look upon as 'our book'. It makes me all the more thankful that it was possible to capture at least some of her wisdom, sanity, godliness and wealth of experience in *Who Walk Alone*. And so I lovingly and humbly acknowledge a debt of inexpressible gratitude, not only for her help in this undertaking, but for all that she taught me from student days onwards.

I gladly pay tribute, too, to my colleague, Anne Long, for all the encouragement and help that she has given; for her generosity in spending so much of her time reading the scripts with painstaking thoroughness, and then discussing them with me. Through her I have learned much, and within the freedom of real trust and love, we have been able to share at a deeply personal level much of what we have experienced as single people. That very sharing has given me confidence to persevere with the book.

The third person who has stood alongside me in real, sympathetic interest throughout the enterprise has been the Rev. Derek W. Allen, Principal of St. Stephen's House, Oxford, and to him I want to express my deep appreciation and gratitude. For his tremendous help (particularly in the chapter on celibacy), for the most generous and carefree way in which he loaned me books and lecture notes, for his kindly hospitality at St. Stephen's House on several occasions when I needed a quiet place in which to write, I should like to record my very sincere thanks. Both my publishers and I hoped that it would be possible to produce a book on the single life which would say something to men as well as women, and for this reason I was more than grateful to have the benefit of a male viewpoint as I wrote. Even more I was immensely thankful to have such warm encouragement from one who is a priest and experienced counsellor for it led me to hope that the book would prove useful to clergy and ministers as well as to single people themselves.

To my typists Mrs. Joan Davies of Ealing, and Miss Pamela Neville of the Baptist Church House, I must also say a special 'Thank you' for such patience, good humour, and an amazing ability to cope with my manuscripts.

The late Rev. W. H. Davies of Ealing was a great support and I owe much to him for his interest in and evaluation of the contents of this book. I valued his judgment very highly and loved him for his generosity, deep personal concern and true Welsh enthusiasm for this venture.

A last and very special word of thanks must go to my long-suffering family for allowing me to descend upon them during the holidays and bury myself in a room among papers and books in an incredibly unsociable way. Without such a sanctuary in which to hide myself, and without their kind ministrations and understanding, the book would never have been completed, for the major part of it was written under their roof. Above all I wish to thank my father and stepmother for the way in which they have always given me complete independence and freedom to enjoy single life so richly and to the full.

Margaret Evening

The poem 'If No One Ever Marries Me' is printed by permission of Garnstone Press; extracts from *Prayers of Life* by Michel Quoist by permission of Gill and Son.

Contents

If No One Ever Marries Me

If no one ever marries me —
And I don't see why they should,
For nurse says I'm not pretty
And I'm seldom very good —

If no one ever marries me
I shan't mind very much;
I shall buy a squirrel in a cage,
And a little rabbit hutch.

I shall have a cottage near a wood,
And a pony all my own,
And a little lamb, quite clean and tame,
That I can take to town..

And when I'm getting really old,
At twenty-eight or nine,
I shall buy a little orphan girl
And bring her up as mine.

LAURENCE ALMA-TADEMAN
c. 1865–1940

From *Realms of Unknown Things* (Garnstone Press).

CHAPTER ONE

The Embarrassing Factor

WE ARE SOMETHING OF AN EMBARRASSMENT, AREN'T WE? I MEAN we single people. People do not know how we feel about our singleness. It is such a delicate subject. They do not like to discuss it with us unless we first 'open up' on the matter; and we are only likely to do that with close friends.

Some single people are obviously discontented. Some try to conceal their longings but do not do it very well. Even those who appear to be contented are a bit of an enigma. Married people sometimes wonder if the efficient man or capable woman who seems to cope so admirably on their own, are really only putting up a façade in order to hide inner loneliness and the ache of incompleteness. Have they really settled happily for singleness, or is it all just a brave front? Can anyone really feel fulfilled without a partner and a home and a family?

Too often it is assumed that true fulfilment can only be found in marriage. Alas, some who get married on that assumption must be sadly disillusioned. There are those too who are so imprisoned in themselves that they would not be able to find fulfilment in marriage or in singleness until they had discovered a real, inward, personal liberation. Fulfilment has to do with filling life full with rich and rewarding experiences, making the most of every opportunity that comes our way and finding joy in all the creative outlets that are open to us.

It is because singleness is a big unknown for so many people (especially those who have married reasonably young) that they hesitate to talk freely about it, while few feel qualified to help the single person who has not learned to cope with life as it has developed. There are Marriage Guidance Counsellors available for those who need help in adjusting to that way of life, but why are there no Single Life Counsellors? Some single people seek advice in the agony columns of women's magazines but, that apart, they have not the known channels of help that exist for their married friends. Perhaps this neglect accounts for the formation of such bodies as the National Council for the Single Woman and her Dependants.[1]

Why is there this reticence? Why *should* there be any embarrassment? How much of it is due to a wholly erroneous idea that the single person has failed in some respect? It is highly unlikely that anyone would say so in as blunt a fashion as that, but, deep down, is this what people think? Judging by the sensitivity of some single people themselves, *they* feel this. Either they have failed or life has cheated them.

It is often assumed that a woman is more sensitive about this than a man simply because she has to be on the receiving end of any proposal. The man has the initiative, so, as far as a single man is concerned, he has but to hurry up and ask a girl to marry him and he is all right. We need not waste too much sympathy on him, we argue. Perhaps, however, the problem for men is *more* acute than for women. The very fact that the initiative *is* with him makes it all the more galling if he feels unable to relate to women. It might constitute a severe threat to him if he suspects that the reason for this is because he is unattractive to the opposite sex. We sometimes jokingly talk of the male ego, but what a blow it takes if he cannot achieve

[1] National Council for the Single Woman and Her Dependants, 166 Victoria St., London S.W.1.

success here when other men seem to find it so easy! They have
but to snap their fingers and the girls come running. Some of
them seem positive Casanovas. They have a steady succession
of girl friends from whom to make their final choice and there
are those who cannot resist trying out their charm on women
folk, even after marriage. By comparison, there must be quite
a lot of lonely single men. Maybe we do not think of *them*
sobbing out their hearts in frustration, but the ache must
nevertheless be there. The fear of rejection is terrible and some
are afraid to venture too far into a relationship because of this
fear. Maybe with a very understanding, gentle and patient
woman they could be helped to overcome it, but it is not
always easy for a woman to get that near to them.

For many single women, singleness brings a deep-seated,
hidden yet agonising sense of failure. The majority of women
in their twenties probably imagine and hope that they will
marry, but if by the late twenties or early thirties there is no
sign of a husband-to-be, they begin to panic. 'Am I going to be
a spinster after all?' they ask themselves adding without
saying it: 'one of that dreaded brigade'. They begin to wonder
if there is some component part missing in their make-up. Do
they lack the necessary magnetism to attract men? They are
genuinely puzzled. After all they dress as attractively as their
married sisters (sometimes more so because they are able to
afford it). Without being unduly conceited, they reckon that
they are blessed with equally good looks. They enjoy life and
are full of fun. They talk intelligently, and, as far as they know,
they have looked into all the possible causes that, according to
the T.V. keep men at bay. They neither suffer from B.O. nor
bad breath. So what has gone wrong? A girl may even have a
number of men friends who seem to like her company, but none
of them thinks of her as a marriage partner.

This sense of failure is only aggravated by well-meaning
family and friends who teasingly ask: 'When are you going to
get married?' or 'Your turn next!' as they stand chatting at the
wedding breakfast of a luckier friend. Such comments simply

confirm for the girl the feeling that this is what everyone expects of her. If she does not get herself a husband somehow, she is going to be a great disappointment to her parents. They want to see her settled in her own home. They long to be proud grandparents.

A group of young divorcees was once asked why they thought their marriages had broken up after a relatively short time. Almost all of them admitted that they had rushed into marriage too quickly 'because we were afraid of being left on the shelf, and we didn't want to disappoint our parents', they said.

We like to think that we are enlightened in these days, but have we really outgrown the Victorian stigma on singleness? Are the social pressures to get married still there? One contemporary journalist[1] has written:

If statistics mean anything, marriage is the most popular way of life. Almost everyone takes to it at some time or another. Those who stay outside the conjugal fold tend to be blamed or pitied and I think it may be these attitudes of the majority which create most of the minority's problems.

Everyone of my generation (people aged between fifty and sixty) will remember the mockery and commiseration which used to be poured out on old maids. I know when I told my mother I wanted to be a 'career girl' because I hated housework and had no longing for children, she said in horrified tones: 'But you wouldn't want to be an *old maid*!' as if I were proposing to catch leprosy. Her viewpoint was shared by all our female acquaintances, who said flatly that no girl could possibly be happy without a husband and family, though among themselves there were several to whom a husband and family had brought little but trouble.

Is there still something in the climate of our thinking that fosters this sense of failure in some single people? Anyone counselling a single person needs to encourage them to look

[1] Evelyn Home, *Personal Problems Today.*

positively at life, to settle for the present reality and not to waste valuable energy living in a fantasy world of day-dreams. But this will not work if there is still a lurking feeling in the minds of married people that singleness has to do with failure. All such false notions *must* be swept away if single people are to look upon their way of life as quite as satisfactory and fulfilling as that of marriage.

Few would be so unkind as to refer blatantly to singleness as failure, but sometimes, in unguarded moments, people betray a tiny legacy of the old Victorian view. One very lonely spinster was sending out all sorts of cries for help—frequent minor illnesses, electrical faults and plumbing problems in the home, and a host of other things that brought people running. When in one of her not infrequent weeping sessions she sobbed out her loneliness, a married friend said: 'Well, what can *I* do about it? It's not my fault that she has no husband.' I suspect that this says more about the married woman's inability to cope with the situation than the single woman's problem, but why has the word 'fault' crept in or, perhaps more accurately, *slipped out* at all? It must have been lurking somewhere in the back of her mind. 'Fault' . . . 'Failure' . . . These words should never be placed in juxtaposition to 'singleness'. They simply do not feature in this business at all.

As a matter of statistics, some people *have* to remain single. There rarely seems to be an equal division of men and women. The holocaust of two world wars was bound to leave a large group of single women in the Western world for a period of time at any rate. Dr. Francis Schaeffer has even suggested[1] that in our overpopulated and underfed world, Christians might like to regard the single state as the norm and marriage as abnormal.

We all want success and hate the idea of failure. It is possible to be a success in marriage and a success in single life, a failure in marriage and a failure in single life. Most of us know a mixture of both. Success has to do with what we *make* of the

[1] Francis Schaeffer, *The Mark of the Christian* (Hodder and Stoughton).

opportunities that come to us. We are not responsible for the fact that some opportunities never come our way.

The majority of those who are single are so because they have never given or received a proposal of marriage—if we can be perfectly honest about the situation. But we should also bear in mind that some have consciously and deliberately declined marriage because of family duties or religious loyalties. To accept this form of self-denial does not necessarily eliminate loneliness and longing, but certainly the word 'failure' could never be applied to such cases.

Sometimes married people fear that they have failed their single friends by not making sufficient efforts to find suitable partners for them. However deep their concern, however sincere their intentions, married folk really must exercise the utmost caution in any attempts to link people together. Even if they are incorrigible match-makers, they cannot do much more than throw two people into each other's company—and that will not *always* be appreciated. Single people do not usually like to think that others are scheming on their behalf. Moreover it can have very serious consequences. It is possible for married people so to enjoy their own married bliss that they feel sorry that their single friends are missing out on it. So by a few artful devices and well-meaning plans they try and engineer a relationship which would never have evolved normally. If such a friendship should lead on to marriage, but a none too happy one, think what a responsibility the match-makers carry!

We are constantly coming up against examples of frustration and disappointment which should remind us how very careful we have to be in sowing seeds of hope. It may be fascinating to tamper with magnetic poles in a physics lesson and cause iron filings to dance around in exciting patterns at our bidding, but in matters of human relationships, it is better to leave the magnetism to operate naturally.

One of the reasons why Dr. Schaeffer's suggestion of a

solution to our world population problem could never succeed is that men and women have a fundamental need of each other in partnership. The majority find this need met in marriage. We speak of our 'other halves'; in other words, marriage brings, for most people, a sense of completeness.

Ted Hughes, in one of his poems about Crow, speaks of the image of the Son of God in man only being complete in the union of man and woman. The monster Crow sees the worm who is the Son of God and cuts him in half. He pushes one half into the empty shell of man's body, and the other half into the woman. These two halves ache to come together again and find union. It is a valid reminder that the image of God is not to be found in man or woman, but in their complementary relationship.

Gilbert Russell in *Men and Women*[1] has described the need for partnership in similar terms:

> Mankind is made man-woman: the great tree is split at the root. God at the instant of creation, divided the race in two. 'Male and female created he them.' From this great wound the body of man aches and will ache to the end. Sex is the standing problem which can never be merely 'solved'. It is set in the flesh and blood and the quick matter of life and mind, and can only be healed. The wound is healed in marriage—in every marriage; but in no marriage perfectly; and in some hardly at all.

There is truth in this, but it is not the whole truth. The wound may also be healed in the complementariness of the sexes, in friendships outside marriage, in working partnerships, in spiritual bonds; not wholly healed of course for, in some cases, the healing is only minimal. Nevertheless what there is, is healing. We shall look at some of these possibilities as we go along.

In all the discussion on partnership, and our fundamental

[1] Gilbert Russell, *Men and Women* (S.C.M. Press), pp. 15–16.

need of it, however, it is essential that we do not overlook the reverse side of the coin. Whether we are married or single, male or female, old or young, there is a sense in which each of us *walks alone*. In the current jargon, we are all asking 'Who am I?' and seeking to 'find our identities'. It may be in relationship to others that we begin to find ourselves but there is that about our selfhood which is alone and individual, sacred and inviolate. It is alone that we enter the world, and alone that we leave it. And ultimately it is alone that we must stand before God, our Judge and Father. Our relationships in this life either enable us to walk that path freely, creatively, joyously and positively or they weigh us down with the chains of fear, repression, anger and rejection, sometimes bringing us to a standstill. At other times we are released in such a way that we are nearer flying than walking!

Not only do we need to recognise all this. We must learn to welcome it and rejoice in it. Indeed if we are able to accept and enjoy our 'aloneness', then the particular circumstances in which we find ourselves (single or married) become for us not a straitjacket but a framework for positive living. Therefore, since we all 'walk alone' in one respect, it may be that this book will have something to say to all sorts and conditions of men and women.

CHAPTER TWO

To What Purpose Is This Waste?

I want to love, Lord,
I need to love.
All my being is desire;
My heart,
My body
      yearn in the night towards an unknown love.
My arms thrash about and I can seize on no object for
      my love.
I am alone and want to be two.
I speak, and no one is there to listen.
I live, and no one is there to share my life.
Why be so rich and have no one to enrich?
Where does this love come from?
Where is it going?
I want to love, Lord,
I need to love.[1]

MICHEL QUOIST HAS GIVEN US THIS PRAYER CALLED
'To Love'—the prayer of an adolescent, but it could well be
the prayer of many a person who has long left their adolescence
behind. Next to the problem of inner loneliness comes the
problem of how to cope with sexual gifts and energies, and the

[1] Michel Quoist, 'To Love' from *Prayers of Life* (Gill & Son).

finding of a proper outlet for them. No one can presume to give all the answers for no one knows them!

If we believe that God made us as we are with all our bodily appetites, then we cannot suppose that our hunger for sexual activity and satisfaction is any more sinful than our desire for food when we are hungry and sleep when we are tired. Yet so often single people are desperately ashamed of their sexual longings and feel they are abnormal and evil and need to be repressed. That they should *never* be. Repression is no answer. It is only a temporary evasion.

Even if we accept that they are perfectly good, God-given instincts and desires, what are we supposed to do with them if we have no partner? In most normal, healthy single people the desires are just as strong as in married people. Moreover the stronger the personality, the stronger the instincts usually are. If this is recognised realistically, it will perhaps help married people to appreciate the kind of conversations that are helpful and those that are not.

In mixed company do not divide people into 'marrieds' and 'singles', but keep conversation and discussion general. To make deliberate exclusions, as though single people are a different species, is not only hurtful but rude. On the other hand, it could be equally thoughtless of married people to discuss the intimacies of their sexual relationships with those who are single. If someone starts talking about the superb meal they had at a hotel at a time when you are feeling hungry, you can always say: 'Don't talk to me about food, I'm hungry!' Most would feel disinclined to say the same when it is a case of sexual hunger. Single people are often very reluctant to admit that such a hunger even exists. The gift of sex within marriage is something to be greatly enjoyed. It can provide fun and laughter, as well as deep tenderness and intense joy. Within the single life, sexual longings and attempts to satisfy them often bring shame and guilt.

For the bachelor the hunger may be fairly persistent, with perhaps the occasional upsurge, but for the woman with the rhythmic, menstrual cycle there are peaks of desire—usually twice a month. These can be times of acute inner conflict. Her body is so designed that its hormonal activity increases sexual desire so that conception may be possible if intercourse takes place. But it is not going to take place, and she is not going to conceive, so there occurs what some have called 'nature's monthly disappointment'. (It isn't only nature that is disappointed!) The extent of the desire varies enormously from person to person, and from month to month, according to general health and the extent of a person's commitments and activities. For the Christian struggling to live a life of purity in thought as well as deed, it may well be a case of the spirit being willing, but the flesh being not simply weak, but *designed to work in the opposite direction.*

'But surely we don't let our biology govern us!' someone says. To a great extent, we do. If we are hungry we eat, and if we are weary we rest. If we are tense and emotionally worn out, we cry and if we are starved of oxygen we faint. We can gain sufficient mastery over the body to fast, sometimes for long periods. Some have kept vigils of prayer all night. Others, through yoga and breath-control, can do amazing feats with the body. But these are only temporary denials, for there is at the end that which will ultimately satisfy the particular bodily need. The single person must learn to live with sexual appetites knowing that they may never be fully satisfied. So what can they do?

Some may rush to identify themselves with the lover in a romantic novel or in a film – which is neither particularly comforting nor realistic. Some will find relief in masturbation. Some experience involuntary orgasms either in dreams or during the day—and are often embarrassed or guilt-ridden about that. Some will turn to work and use up the energy and drive in a massive output of whatever their line happens to be. All of this may be the experience of the married person too, but for them there are some proper outlets for the sexual energies, even if they are not able to enjoy as rich a sexual life as they would like.

It has been argued that it is so much harder for the widow or widower, having known the satisfaction of sexual union, to have to do without it on the death of their partner. Some feel it is easier for the single person to do without what he or she has never had. But one wonders. It is impossible to generalise for so much depends upon the individual. It may be possible to argue like that over pit ponies who are not aware that light exists. It hardly applies to those whose instincts and appetites are fully recognised and who daily mix with those who can properly express their love in many ways, including sex.

Because sex is a necessarily powerful force, its importance probably becomes exaggerated for those to whom it is denied. The single person knows in theory that sex is only one part of marriage; an important part of course, but not all-important. It is very hard, however, to be satisfied with that argument when oestregen is being pumped round the body (female at any rate), and is doing its work effectively!

Perhaps it is helpful to have some elementary knowledge of the biology of the body. For those who suffer from pre-menstrual tension, it helps to know that there are biological reasons for the irritability and bad temper. It does not, of course, cure them simply to know the cause, but at least they can be specially alert and avoid the occasions and circumstances that are likely to aggravate the tensions during those days. They can ensure that certain protective measures are taken, such as relaxing hot baths, early nights and no undue exertion or strain. It may sound ridiculous to talk in terms of gearing your reading and T.V. viewing to the menstrual cycle, but the old adage 'Feed a cold and starve a fever' may have something relevant to say here. If we know the times when sexual desire may increase and possibly become overwhelming, then we can take deliberate steps to starve it; that is if we really do want to keep things in proportion and enjoy our sexuality in a positive and realistic way.

Some have recommended prayer as a good antidote. I believe in absolute honesty before God, so it is good to come to

Him and offer yourself in all your confusion saying; 'Here I am God, as you designed me. Sin and disobedience to your in-structions may have upset the balance of things, but I need to love and to be loved. Show me the way through which all this energy can be re-directed, and then teach me to laugh at myself for getting things so out of proportion.'

To laugh at sex helps to scale down its importance. Honesty helps because God knows and understands anyway. 'He knoweth our frame.' Jesus was 'tempted in all points like as we are, yet without sin'. Think of the boundless love, compassion, tenderness and gentleness of Jesus Christ. Did he never long to be on the receiving end? Did he never ache to find his own tenderness reciprocated? It must have been a moment of intense joy for him to receive that outward, visible, tangible expression of love from Mary when she poured her precious ointment over his feet. And then the unfeeling, uncomprehend-ing onlooker had to tarnish the moment by talking about the waste of it all. To what purpose was this waste? The act was almost sacramental. It was love ministering to love in a material way.

Besides honesty in prayer, there should also be *thanksgiving*. It is important to recognise that sexuality is a gift, a part of our God-given inheritance and therefore a cause for much thanksgiving. When there are deep inner stirrings of sexual desire, we might utter a profound 'Thank God' for this renewed evidence of our manhood or womanhood. Every time there comes the somersault in the stomach and the quickening of the pulse, it is good to know that that part of our being has not completely shrivelled up and died. It is a real opportunity to turn temptation into thanksgiving.

The recommendation that prayer is an antidote to unruly passions should perhaps carry a warning too. It may not always be the right answer in the face of this *particular* tempta-tion. Some hold that passion that leads to spiritual fervour and passion that leads to sexual activity stem from a common root. Although they run side by side in their separate channels, there are times when it seems as though a kind of spiritual osmosis takes place. The dividing wall between the channels is thin enough for the two energies to get mixed up, hence the strange phenomenon, observed sometimes by missionaries, of a higher incidence of sexual immorality following a religious revival. Fervent prayer often heightens our awareness and longing for love in all directions and not only Godwards. So it should. It is one of the elementary lessons of prayer that it not only expresses love but engenders it too.

Jesus taught his disciples to 'Bless them that persecute you and pray for them that despitefully use you' because that was the surest way of bringing them to the point where they would be able to 'love their enemies'. True contemplation of God is never a selfish thing and often leads to great social activity and service to one's stricken fellow beings. 'Love must be made real in act' wrote T. S. Eliot. Perhaps one of our clearest examples of this in recent years has been the well-known work of Mother Theresa who has, literally, scooped up dying humanity from the streets of Calcutta and loved and cared for the desperately needy she has found there.

At the risk of contradiction, I would say that prayer may not always be the best first step to take in the face of this particular temptation. It might be better to get out and be with other people for a while, or become absorbed in an exacting piece of work. If by a deliberate act of the will, all the longing to love and be loved *can* be directed towards others in need, then this can be one of the highest forms of intercession. Perhaps one of the reasons why intercession sometimes seems rather dreary and unrealistic is that not enough of our emotional energy and imaginative love are poured into it. This is a form of service in which all Christians should be involved, but the single Christian may have a special contribution to make just because of the channelling of these strong urges to love.

It will be noticed that I have stuck to the word *channelling* rather than the word *sublimation*. So much nonsense has been talked about sublimation that many people react strongly to the idea. It *is* an unfortunate word because sub-anything seems to suggest a pushing under, something below standard, a second best. Even 'channelling' is not wholly appropriate. It suggests that one channel is blocked and the energies have been completely rerouted, whereas most single people want to know how to keep that channel open and learn to enjoy their sexuality even without a particular lover. They want to enjoy it in such a way that it is not a burden to them but a delight.

For healthy Christian living, we ought to be able to rejoice in our bodies' senses and physical delights without regarding them as occasions of sin. This they can be, but they need not be so. Many Christians today (round the middle-age bracket) have distinct gnostic tendencies in their attitude to the body. They still regard matter as though it were wholly evil, and the body as something from which we are always longing to set the spirit free, as though it were a caged bird. We will never entirely rid ourselves of this dualistic way of thinking unless we can come to see the body as a mode or expression of existence. Roger Mehl makes this point in his book *Society and Love*.[1]

> It is high time that Christian theology developed an ethic of the body, abandoning thereby all traces of puritanism and relics of gnostic Hellenism . . . Far from the body being, as Plato would have it, 'the soul's tomb', it is rather the intermediary by which others become real to me, and through which I become real to others, the means whereby loneliness is banished as well as the means by which and within which I protect my most intimate self.

It is possible to enjoy one's sexuality simply in the company of friends of the opposite sex. Frustrations are diminished if one is able to have a healthy working relationship with them. Happy are those who work in a mixed staff room or office. The single

[1] Roger Mehl, *Société et Amour* (Geneva).

woman, for example, can greatly enjoy the little courtesies of men that make her feel a woman. It is wholly natural and right that she should enjoy their admiration of her choice of clothes or her figure or her hair. She is not setting out to lure and attract them wrongfully if she takes care over her appearance. She should cultivate a sense of taste and colour and beauty, and attempt to dress in such a way that the outside appearance approximates as nearly as possible to her inner being. She can revel in the kind of conversation that will be sparked off by mixed company, which is often far more creative and interesting than that between men and men, or women and women. She can enjoy the outward signs of affection—the embrace, the kiss, the taking of the hand—purely and fearlessly given by men friends who are quite sure that she is *not* a hungry tigress waiting to devour them, but to whom she is related in mutual trust.

MASTURBATION

To what purpose was this waste? No chapter dealing with the subject of coping with sexual desires would be adequate if it said nothing about masturbation, particularly since it is a *very* common problem. One set of figures has recorded that 90 per cent of men and 75 per cent of women masturbate (but perhaps the men were more honest!). Most counsellors know that this is something which bothers many single people. Many can never bring themselves to ask for help, while those who do seek help usually have to summon every scrap of courage to do it. One priest has said that he always felt that when masturbation had been confessed, he had really heard all, because that was almost always the last thing to be mentioned.

This human activity has been given much publicity recently. In one sense, it is good that there can be more openness about it. At least most of the old wives' tales and silly notions threatening possible blindness, barrenness or impotence because of it, have been cleared out of the way. But for many single people it still remains a 'problem' because they cannot practise masturbation without a sense of guilt. Why is there guilt?

There are doctors who say it is a wholly harmless form of sexual relief. There are counsellors who feel sure that there is a proper place for it, particularly where fuller forms of sexual expression are denied—for example, soldiers or sailors whose duties mean long separation from their wives, or the husband who cannot make love to his wife on account of her ill-health or near confinement. Similarly, they would even recommend it as a satisfactory form of relief to single people, suggesting that it should be practised with the same degree of chastity that is required in marriage. Sexual greed in either state is a sign that there is something wrong. It still remains true, however, that there are few Christians who can practise masturbation with a clear conscience. Allowing for all sorts of conditioning processes and dire threats in childhood, are there any other reasons why this guilt should be felt?

Is it because it is selfish? Love is always a leaving of oneself to go towards others, but this is a form of *self* indulgence. While it seems wholly understandable for the husband and wife who are separated for some reason or other, to engage in it, nevertheless, it is not a coming together in union. It is not the mutual giving of love and pleasure. It is the forms of *self* indulgence (which may or may not include bodily activities) that St. Paul lists as those works of the flesh which war against the spirit (Galatians 5:19–21).

Is it because masturbation is less than reality that guilt arises? For the Christian whose longing for God leads him nearer and nearer to Reality, *anything* less than reality in any sphere of life pulls him back from his desired goal. In the journey towards God, there has to be a continual banishing of all that is unreal both in mental and physical activity.

Is it because it is felt to be a form of immaturity? We accept masturbation as fairly normal in children. It is part of growing up for many—an exploring and discovering of the body for some, and for others the meeting of a need for comfort. Does the shame really spring from the knowledge that there is an area of life where one has not grown up?

Or is it because of the mental images and fantasies that usually accompany the act? Dr. Leslie Weatherhead was once asked in public whether masturbation was a sin. His answer was this. 'It depends whether the picture on the screen of the mind at the time could be shown to our Lord without shame.' He enlarges on this a little in his book, *Psychology, Religion and Healing* where he says this:

> Sometimes masturbation is sin, for in repeated imaginative scenes with a prohibited person control is lost, making the sudden actualisation of such a scene a disaster. Habit tracks formed during imaginative scenes carry impulses into regrettable action in actual life if opportunity suddenly offers. At the same time, in many situations, guilt is exaggerated and that exaggerated burden must be removed.

In this he is right. The guilt is often out of all proportion to the act. People are often far less worried by their lying and deceit, their back-biting and jealousy, their laziness and anger, and yet ultimately these are far more destructive. At least masturbation usually has to do with love, even if it is love turned in on itself, or love gone wrong.

There are other times, of course, when it is plainly lustful. Perhaps one should try and find a middle path between the medical opinion and the dictates of conscience and say that there may well be a right place for this kind of relief *at certain times* — in and out of marriage — always recognising that it is less than the best and viewing it as one of those weights which one hopes eventually to lay aside so that progress towards full maturity may be less impeded.

This could certainly be said of one type of masturbation though perhaps it would be helpful, in this discussion, to recognise *two* kinds. There is that which is explosive and urgent, that gives immediate physical relief to a sudden immense build-up of sexual energy. This kind of relief should not carry a huge burden of guilt. It may be regrettable and one may long to find more satisfactory channels for releasing sexual energy, but there needs to be a sense of proportion about what is happening. Like nocturnal emissions or bed wetting, it may bring a good deal of distress and embarrassment but the best way to overcome it is to play down the importance of it.

There is, however, the other kind of masturbation which is not an urgent necessity but a self-indulgent luxury, a deliberate turning away from reality, a way of stimulating or supporting sexual fantasies. In other words, the distinction lies between that activity which is plainly animal and physical with no accompanying pictures in the mind, and that which is certainly physical but which is also strongly mental and imaginative. For let us be clear about this. We may be talking about the bodily symptoms but the battle is in the mind, and it is first and foremostly in the *mind* that it must be fought. Such mental activity may very well involve another person (unbeknown to him or her) in a fantasy relationship that is illicit and possibly dishonouring. And it is no good arguing that 'I am not hurting anyone but myself: this is a purely private act'. We are members one of another even in the sub-strata of thought and imagination. In the teaching of Christ it is clear that we are as accountable for our hidden motives and desires as we are for their outward expression.

It would seem then that this latter form is really the kind of masturbation that must be fought. 'But how?' some will ask, perhaps desperately.

There are no easy answers and no *general* advice. What would be helpful for one, might be quite the opposite for another. I heard of one person who was recommended to take a long, hot, relaxing bath before going to bed. But it was the worst possible advice in that case, for it was the very sight of her own body that caused the upsurge of desire. Another young man told me that a camp leader had suggested going to bed wearing boxing gloves! Enough said!

It may be of some help, however, to consider the following as possible ways of combating this unwanted habit, always realising that they will not help in every case.

On a practical level—don't put the light out until you are ready to drop off to sleep. Read a book (not a romantic one), plan shopping lists, do your accounts, design a dress or plan out co-ordinates, write letters, etc. Do anything that engages the mind until you have reached the point of exhaustion and you are able to fall asleep the minute your head touches the pillow.

For some it may not be a practical possibility to keep a light on, so it may mean mental exercises in the dark. In these circumstances it is helpful to be really physically tired before going to bed. Then if sleep doesn't come immediately, it might help if you go back in memory to some moment of *pure* joy and relive that experience. I hope that doesn't sound like escapism. It is a legitimate use of the gift of memory. Go back to holiday experiences—a mountain walk in clean, fresh air, a swim in warm, blue seas, a promenade concert, or an exciting discovery. Use every imaginative power to conjure up the sights, sounds, smells, feel of fresh air, the taste of different food, the wind in the hair, the lovely burning of a sun tan. These are bodily delights in which there is no shame. If your imagination is going to get to work anyway, make it work the way *you* choose and keep hard at it so that thoughts don't slip off down unscheduled paths.

Most of all, for those in the habit of worship, it may be helpful to go back to some peak moment either in corporate or individual worship—a moment of communion where Heaven touched earth and you joined your praises from an overflowing heart to the Eucharistic praise of the whole church militant and triumphant; a moment of quiet meditation when you touched upon reality; a moment when you made a deep resolve or commitment to our Lord as, for example, in baptism, confirmation, conversion or ordination. Re-affirm those vows, remind yourself of the insights that came to you, and by any and every act of the will, direct your loving towards the God you acknowledged in those experiences. 'Pious claptrap' you may want to say. I hope it is deeply practical advice too. It seems a real way forward to me because surely there are *many* ways in which a spirit of praise and thanksgiving can drive away polluted thoughts and deeds. If masturbation of this sort is largely a matter of self-love, then it is also a spiritual battle and needs to be fought with spiritual weapons.

Hard though it may be, it *is* a help to share the problem with someone else. [Don't fear either the word or the use of it.] It gets the whole thing into perspective and helps to reduce exaggerated guilt-feelings, especially when it is seen that the confidant registers neither embarrassment nor shock. It is such a common part of the human condition, and it is one of the least surprising things to come out in confession, even if it is, as the priest I quoted earlier, said, the last!

After this subject had been discussed in one counselling course, one man went to the counsellor in some distress because he felt there must be something abnormal about him. He had never masturbated!

If any of what has been said seems to be a running away from the heart of the matter, then perhaps the most helpful thing to do would be to penetrate those fantasy relationships and see them for what they really are. Sit up in bed and look at them in a cold, analytical light. It will take considerable will-power, but do it. Try and get right inside the fantasy and inject a bit of reality into it. For example, if the object of the fantasy relationship is someone else's husband, then do the most sensible, if unwelcome, thing at that moment. Think about his wife. Think realistically about her. How do you feel when you meet her? What sort of conflicts are roused by your love for her and your love for her husband? Must these always be in conflict? If not, how can they be resolved? How can you increase your enjoyment of *her* company, as a friend in her own right? And when you have taken a calculated look at the whole situation, pray for her.

For many people the temptation to masturbate comes especially at night. If that is so, then it is worth taking preventive measures during the daytime. In other words, work at satisfactory relationships in ordinary daily contacts. It seems highly likely that if there is a real, enriching input in terms of relationships, the force of the temptation will be reduced, for the hunger for love and comfort and tenderness is being satisfied. It would be very interesting to know if there is a correlation between a sense of well-being and a reduction in masturbation. Much more analytical thinking is therefore needed on this subject. 'What are my needs, and how are they being met?' The needs will certainly include a receiving in friendship but also real opportunities for giving. For it is, of course, these together that constitute the enriching input.

How far can one trace the need to masturbate to feelings of rejection and insecurity? It is certainly true that children often seek it as a form of comfort when they feel insecure. If this is true of the adult and he has experienced God's loving and caring as a reality, then it would surely be helpful to 'call this to remembrance' in the Hebrew sense, i.e. making actual in the present that which was experienced in the past. It must help to take hold of certain promises and go over and over them in the mind *before* the temptation comes. For the moment of transition between temptation and action can often be *very* sudden and there is scarcely time to do battle. Laying hold of the promises God has made about His love for us will bring a sense of conscious security which helps to deal with the unconscious insecurities.

One thing seems certain: 'The love of God is broader than the measure of man's mind and the heart of the Eternal is most wonderfully kind.'[1] It may help people to stop condemning themselves, if they grasp the fact that God is far less harsh with them than they are with themselves.

For the Christian there may be one further point to consider.

[1] F. W. Faber, *Souls of Men, Why Will Ye Scatter?*

We none of us live to ourselves. By our thinking as well as our doing, we can create the kind of ethos in which it is easier or harder for others to sin. Our submission to the invasion of impure thoughts in the kingdom of our minds may make it easier for someone else, who is struggling, to give in. It may be rather like St. Paul and his 'meat offered to idols'. The exercise of restraint is our responsibility, not necessarily because something is sinful but in order to help the weaker brother. Or, as one humps over in bed in resolute inactivity, is there not a sense in which one can share the words of our Lord? 'For their sakes, I sanctify myself?'

To what purpose is this waste of our sexuality? It should never really be thought of as a waste, of course. It may be difficult to handle powerful sexual urges and keep them in their proper place, but none of us would want to be without them. What 'cold fish' we would then be! Some of the most loving and warm-hearted people I know are single and have so much love to give that people cannot help but return it. They are enriched beyond words in the event. The secret is in the story of Mary's extravagant gesture of love. She did not only pour out precious perfume. She poured out her whole self and her love. It was this pouring out in total disregard of self that brought our Lord's commendation: 'She hath done what she could . . . she loved much . . . and for this she will always be remembered.'

CHAPTER THREE

The Risks of Love—With the Same Sex

No love relationship, whether in marriage or the single life, is free from risk. It is, however, one of the marks of maturity to be able to take sensible risks.

A Chinese proverb says: 'It is better to travel and not to arrive than not to have travelled at all.' In the same way it could be said that it is better to have loved and to have made mistakes than never to have loved at all. Some people fear real friendship which involves any degree of intensity or commitment to such an extent that they become incapable of anything more than superficial relationships. That is very sad, for life without true friendship is hardly life at all.

Many years ago I had a dream. It was one of the few coherent dreams that I have ever had, but it was so vivid that even now I can remember the details of it clearly.

In the dream I visited Hell, where the sub-Warden showed me round. To my surprise I was led along a labyrinth of dark, dank passages from which there were numerous doors leading into cells. It was not like Hell as I had pictured it at all. In fact, it was all rather religious and 'churchy'! Each cell was identical. The central piece of furniture was an altar, and before each altar knelt (or, in some cases, were prostrated) greeny-grey spectral figures in attitudes of prayer and adoration. 'But whom are they worshipping?' I asked my guide. 'Themselves' came the reply immediately. 'This is "pure" self-worship. They are feeding on themselves and their own spiritual vitality in a kind of auto-spiritual-cannibalism. That is why they are so sickly looking and emaciated.'

I was appalled and saddened by the row upon row of cells with their non-communicating inmates, spending eternity in solitary confinement, themselves the first, last and only object of worship.

The dream continued . . . but the point germane to our discussion here has been made. According to the teaching of the New Testament, *Heaven is community*. My dream reminded me that *Hell is isolation*.

Just as we are capable of enjoying a foretaste of Heaven in this life, so it is also possible to experience something of Hell on earth. They are deprived people indeed who are without friends (even if it be by their own choice), for they are not only missing out on companionship and are therefore a prey to physical loneliness and isolation, but they are also missing something much more serious.

As children we learn to share our *things* (our toys, our games, our sweets) with our friends. As adults we should be learning to share *ourselves*. Just as children often have a tussle within themselves over the matter of sharing, so there is not always immediate victory for adults. Some are naturally reticent and shy. Others are locked up in themselves for one reason or another, possibly through emotional wounds inflicted in childhood. There are many contributory factors that make one person a 'giving' person and another a 'closed' person. As Jacques Pasquier[1] has pointed out:

The gift of oneself in love is tied to one's own self image and to one's acceptance of this image. Genuine love and

[1] Jacques Pasquier, 'Celibacy and Effective Maturity', in *The Way* (published by the English Jesuits).

self-giving are impossible for someone who has not learnt
from experience that he himself can be loved. It is only
when the individual realises that he is important for someone
else that life takes on meaning. So long as we are strangers to
this experience of being loved for what we are, of being
accepted in our entirety, we remain incapable of genuine
love.

It is a basic rule that when self becomes 'unlocked' and
opens out to give, it will, *in exact proportion*, be able to receive.
Individuals (or a married couple, or a family, or an exclusive
group for that matter) shut up in themselves, not only fail to
give. They cannot receive either. They are therefore, not only
impoverished, but actually stunted in their emotional development. It is in this mutual giving and receiving, the sharing of
insights, news, experiences, joys, wisdom, fun, the questions
that rise from the depths of one's inner being, the mystery of
one's selfhood . . . that we are able to grow.

Ironically, there can be a kind of loving and giving which is
more a meeting of *our* needs than the other person's. That is not
a genuine overflow of love. As someone put it: 'Sometimes I
wear a smiling face and appear outgoing and helpful while
inside there is an angry and protesting heart.'

Norman Pittenger has said:[1]

When we refuse mutuality, so that in our relationships we
seek only to 'get' but not to give or we refuse to receive from
others that which they can give us and which they urgently
desire to give us, we are living without true love. . . . When
we seek to avoid all deep union with others, and are ready
to have only superficial and understanding relationships
with them, making it easy for ourselves to avoid the purification of self which genuine union always demands and
always effects, we are living without true love.

There is a lovely story told of the great Indian mystic, Sadhu

[1] Norman Pittenger, *Time for Consent* (S.C.M. Press), pp. 35, 36.

Sundar Singh.[1] It is in fact a parable about mutuality. When crossing a range of mountains in a heavy snowstorm he was joined by a Tibetan who was afraid of going alone. The cold was so intense that they had already begun to despair of reaching their destination alive, when they saw a man who had slipped down a slope of snow some thirty feet below the path, lying there unconscious. The Sadhu asked his companion to help him carry the man to the village. The Tibetan told him that he was a fool to try and help another when he could barely save himself, so left him and hurried on ahead.

The Sadhu would not hear of abandoning the helpless man so, he went down the slope and struggled to lift the unconscious form on to his shoulders. Tottering forward under the weight, he set off to follow in the same direction that the other man had taken. After he had been battling against the wind and the snow for another two hours or so, he began to feel warmer. The exertion of carrying the stranger was causing his own blood to circulate more freely. More wonderful still, the heat generated from his own body began to warm that of the frozen man and, although he was still too weak to walk, he regained consciousness. The Sadhu trudged on, finding his task easier as time went by. He realised that it was the mutual giving and receiving of warmth that kept them both alive. Suddenly they saw a mound in the tracks ahead of them. As they got closer, they found it was the frozen, lifeless body of the Tibetan.

Sometimes we overlook the fact that what we are given in friendship helps to make us what we are. How could we begin to unravel all the influences that have gone into the very fibre of our beings? How could we begin to assess all the enriching input that friendship has brought?

One of the great joys of friendship is that it is something which is freely chosen. We do not choose our parents. We have no control over the influences of our childhood environment. Sometimes those influences need to be unravelled, perhaps

[1] Streeter and Appasamy, *The Sadhu*.

with psychotherapeutic help, in which a person is 'blocked' and longs to be released into full maturity. But we do have a choice where our friends are concerned. C. S. Lewis[1] speaks of it as the 'least natural of Loves. . . . Without Eros none of us would have been begotten and without Affection none of us would have been reared; but we can live and breed without Friendship. . . .'

It was this 'non-natural' quality in friendship which was so exalted in ancient and medieval times and

has come to be made light of in our own . . . Nature and emotion and the body were feared as dangers to our souls, or despised as degradations of our human status. Inevitably that sort of love was most prized which seemed most independent, or even defiant, of mere nature. Affection and Eros were too obviously connected with our nerves, too obviously shared with the brutes. You could feel these tugging at your guts and fluttering in your diaphragm. But in Friendship—in that luminous, tranquil, rational world of relationships freely chosen—you got away from all that. This alone of all loves seemed to raise you to the level of gods or angels . . . Friendship is a relation between men at their highest level of individuality.

A variety of friends will inevitably mean a variety of input. This makes for richness. A person with many friends is blessed not only because he need never be lonely, but also because his life is brightened by the whole range of colours within the spectrum of friendship. No one person can give us all that we need emotionally—not even a husband or a wife. As Laura Hutton has said: 'no friendship should carry the whole charge of someone's emotional life.'[2] Sadly we have probably all met the sort of husband or wife who would like this to be so, and who

---

[1] C. S. Lewis, *The Four Loves* (Fontana), pp. 56–57.
[2] Laura Hutton, *The Single Woman: Her Adjustment to Life and Love* (Barrie & Rockliff).

has wrapped their jealousy and protection around their partner
like clinging ivy, effectively preventing the growth of the other's
true self. It can be just as true of friends as married couples, of
course. Whatever the commitment, a truly loving relationship
should bring increasing liberty and expansiveness—not a sense
of imprisonment and bondage. Possessiveness is a very ugly
ingredient in any relationship.

PARTICULAR FRIENDSHIPS

The normal pattern of relationships is to have a number of
friends, but only a few really close friends. The level of friendship of which C. S. Lewis speaks above is that of a particular
rather than a general nature. Healthy single people will want to
have many friends, married and single, male and female, and will
not want to concentrate all their emotional energies upon one
special friend. But that is not to say that there will not be *some*
special friends within the wider group. For 'one of the sensible
risks that maturity is able to take is a certain selectiveness in
one's relationships. It would be simply unrealistic to believe
that anyone can enter into friendship with everyone around
them.'[1]

Perhaps it is particularly necessary for the single person to have
some close friends, not only for the sake of companionship,
but in order to give a sense of belonging. It can never be that
utter belonging that is one of the joys of marriage, but nevertheless it can be an intimate sharing which makes possible both
a deeper discovery of oneself and a going out to the other in
reckless self abandonment.

C. S. Lewis has described the difference in the particularity
of the married relationship and that of friends in this way.
'Lovers are always talking to one another about their love;
friends hardly ever about their friendship. Lovers are normally
face to face; friends side by side, absorbed in some common
interest.'[2] If we continue to think along the lines of this analogy,

[1] Jacques Pasquier, 'Celibacy and Effective Maturity'.
[2] C. S. Lewis, *The Four Lovers*.

it is easy to see that a third person would be an intrusion and distraction for the lovers for, face to face, they have eyes only for each other. But a third, or a fourth or fifth friend who comes to fix his eyes on the common interest does not get in the way but adds to the mutual enjoyment. While this is a helpful differentiation, we must not press the analogy too far for it is not the whole truth.

There are, of course, times when friends wish to be 'à deux', and the arrival of anyone else *is* an intrusion. What both want at that moment is a one-to-one encounter — and there is nothing improper or unhealthy in that! There are some aspects of our personality that we only reveal under those conditions. To do it within a group would be almost impossible. Perhaps we could say then that there are those times for friends as well as for married people when they turn and look at each other, for they recognise in each other a deep need to matter, to belong, to enter into communion. In such a relationship the masks can be thrown off, the poses abandoned, the fear of being known cast away, and the two can know as full a measure of acceptance as is possible at that moment. Of course, the turning to look at each other is not a position that they can or should maintain. It is not something which (by sacred vow) is kept exclusively for each other alone, but it is a ministry which enables both to see something of the meaning of God's acceptance of us in spite of, and because of, His knowledge of us.

Relationships where there can be that level of self-exposure and sharing, are deeply satisfying, but the safeguard is always there in the acceptance of the right of others to stand in a different but equally close relationship to the friend. Only in marriage is there the right to a unique relationship of belonging. Other loving must always be inclusive to some degree. As soon as one friend becomes possessive towards another, the death knell of that relationship has begun to toll. For possessiveness confines and encloses, till like a moth in a jam jar, the 'other' beats his wings to break loose and be free again.

Why is it then that particular friendships have often been disliked and distrusted by 'the herd'? Why are they sometimes frowned upon by headmasters, headmistresses and superiors of religious communities? Why is it that people often feel uneasy when they see a close and strong bond developing between two friends, particularly if they are of the same sex?

There is, as there has always been, the fear of homosexuality. Even if it is quite clear that friends are not engaging in homosexual practices, there is often the gnawing suspicion that this is a relationship that is really homosexual by nature. Religious communities have sometimes feared particular friendships because exclusiveness could war against the very spirit of community. A community is not made up of a lot of little knots but of one unbroken skein showing neither divisions nor clumsy 'joinings up'.

Apart from these rather specialised fears, however, are there any other kinds of unease about special friendships that are at all valid? Are we not safe if we bear in mind that friendship cannot mean belonging exclusively to another, that that is marriage? It cannot mean being owned by another. That is slavery. But, it can mean being specially drawn to another and open to him or her to a greater degree than to anyone else. There are those secret hopes and fears, the intolerable burdens of failure and sin that can be shared. There are the moments of absurdity and fooling you are not ashamed to enjoy. There are worries about work loads, minor ailments, family misunderstandings that can be dragged out into the open. One does not necessarily want to air these publicly, but it is not necessary to bear them alone.

Florence Allshorn helped me to see how common it is for people, especially single people, to walk an unnecessarily lonely path of anxiety. With her eminent good sense, she warned missionary candidates that far too often single women will put up with all sorts of small things that *together* make a heavy burden, simply because they feel they cannot bother anyone else with their little problems. There are, of course, the neurotics who fuss about every minor disorder, but there are even more the stoics who try to ignore them.

Perhaps there is nowhere where this is more clearly demonstrated than on the mission field. It is not the broken legs or pneumonia that really are the 'last straw'. It is the accumulation of discomforts such as skin eruptions and constipation, ingrowing toenails and mouth ulcers, that one accepts with a grin-and-bear it attitude and never dreams of mentioning to other people because they seem so trifling. Yet friends will not only help us to laugh at our worries if they are silly. They will often march us to the doctor or dentist if we are ignoring nature's warning signals (however slight they may be). Which of us does not need to be taken in hand by our friends from time to time?

Of course there is a valid unease in the sense that all relationships carry the risks of love—and the special friendship is not an exception. But it can be a good risk. Closeness has its dangers but also its immense comforts.

Archbishop Lang once wrote something to the effect that 'in the loneliness of his bachelor life his great need was not for friends, of whom he had plenty, any more than it was for work, of which he had too much. It was for that old, simple, human thing—someone in daily nearness to love.'

How special then can a relationship be without falling into error?

Not so special that any other friend is neglected or considered a nuisance.

Not so special that one can really only enjoy the times when one is alone with that person.

Not so special that jealousy creeps in.

Not so special that one is constantly re-living memories of the past, or eagerly anticipating meetings of the future, never able to enjoy to the full what J. P. de Caussade has called 'the sacrament of the present moment'.[1]

[1] J. P. Caussade, S.J., *Self Abandonment to Divine Providence* (Burns, Oates & Washbourne).

Not so special that the prospect of separation at some future date is like a sword of Damocles hanging over the relationship.

Not so special that it affects normal relationships with the opposite sex.

Not so special that the two lives become inseparably intertwined. In marriage there is a fusion of two personalities expressed in the one-flesh union. In friendship the two personalities run side by side, the more enriched for knowing each other, mutually strengthened by their closeness but nevertheless separate, for separation will have to come.

Often these special friendships begin when people are thrown together, not necessarily by choice but by necessity. A common responsibility may bring them into close bonds, for example the shared leadership of a Scout troop or a Guide Company, membership of an orchestra or choir with regular practices, or the running of various church organisations. It is not unusual for students to find themselves involved in close relationships. Where it is a case of living together in a hall of residence, sharing a general purposes room, talking endlessly over cups of coffee about important as well as inconsequential things, all combined with the loneliness of 'the first time away from home' and involvement in a vast institution, it is very easy for exclusive friendships to form.

It is when a friendship crosses the boundary from 'special' to 'exclusive' that all the red warning lights should start flashing. I do not mean simply that a friendship may become what people sometimes describe as 'unhealthy'. I am suggesting that it is actually *wrong*. For true love is outgoing and inclusive, even in those deepest and most unique bonds.

ON THE MISSION FIELD

One potential trouble spot as far as such relationships are concerned, and I do not apologise for returning to it, is the mission field. Here I deliberately lean heavily on my own missionary experience. When we give missionaries a great send-off at their valedictory services, we are not always aware of the emotional dangers (as well as the physical and spiritual dangers) into which we are sending them. The very nature of the mission station set-up gives rise to difficulties at times.

Take, for example, a fairly typical situation where there are two married couples and two single women. Nowadays, single women are allowed to live alone if they wish to, and if there is sufficient accommodation. Quite often, however, it isn't possible to spare a whole house to one person, and the two single people are allocated a house between them. They have not chosen each other for companionship; they just find themselves appointed to the same station. This can be a very difficult situation if the two do not get on particularly well. They might not have done so in their own country, let alone in a foreign field with all the additional strains of climate, overwork, loneliness and frustration. They cannot escape each other for there may be little opportunity to meet other missionaries apart from those on their own station and yet they cannot allow the scandal of quarrelling to hinder their work and witness.

On the other hand, the two single folk may get on very well indeed. They may enjoy each other's company and their pattern of life fits in smoothly. Everyone heaves a sigh of relief and says 'Thank God for that!' But then later there come gnawing doubts. Are they getting on just too well? Is this going to be all right, or could it end in something of a scandal? It is possible to see how a potentially dangerous situation is developing.

The two single folk share a kitchen, so they eat their meals together and naturally share the housekeeping expenses. It is only a small step from this to sharing most expenses. I have even known cases where friends have kept a common purse. They enjoy home-making and entertaining and have tastes that dovetail perfectly, so they buy their fitments, furniture, curtains and pictures jointly (that makes it difficult to separate them). They share a car ('it would be foolish and unnecessarily expensive to run two when we usually go everywhere together') which means that it is difficult for either to take a trip away without the other. If they did so, one would be conscious of leaving the other without transport. Nor is it easy to cultivate separate friendships for they are nearly always invited out as a pair, since they themselves do their entertaining jointly. Soon not only finances are shared but letters are shared too. All the news from home is read out to the partner. The respective families at home begin to address their letters to both women. Each family feels it has an adopted daughter. Links are made between the two sets of parents at home. How lovely that such a bond has brought them together! And so it is, if the friends can walk the tightrope of risk without tumbling off.

Since they are sharing a home, finances, work, car, family news, what more right and proper than that they should share in prayer together. This is fine, and can be a tremendous source of strength and mutual encouragement, *provided* there is also a separateness before God. Shared prayer must be an addition to private prayer and not a substitute for it.

All of this could probably happen in the case of two single men, though there are few such cases of bachelors sharing on the mission field (they never seem to remain bachelors long enough for things to develop as far as that!). Equally, all of this could happen in one's home country as much as abroad, but at home it is not usually by *force* of circumstances. People do have more choice in the matter of sharing a home, and more opportunities for mixing in a wider circle.

'But what is wrong in this kind of situation?' you may well ask. As one single woman missionary once protested: 'If we were always quarrelling and couldn't get on together, our married colleagues would frown at that and call it a scandal. If we haunted their houses, they would complain of that. When we get on well and are very fond of each other, they have their doubts about that too. You just can't please them!' She had a point, of course!

It might perhaps help to consider the following points:

4

The first is that, however much two people love each other in this sort of situation, they are NOT *married to each other.* They may try and simulate the kind of home life of a married couple by sharing life very fully, but it is still not marriage. It cannot be a union, but only co-habitation—even if it is a very loving co-habitation. Nor can there be any pledge of permanence. However much two friends may wish to stay together and plan to spend their lives together, it is not always possible. In the missionary situation there are furloughs which cannot always, if ever, be taken together. What if someone else is appointed to take over the work of the absent missionary and to take her place in the single women's house? Will she be welcomed or resented? Will it be difficult not to make comparisons? Will the absent missionary on furlough feel fearful that her place has been usurped every time the newcomer's name is mentioned in letters? Is this going to lead to an acute and miserable battle with jealousy? What if there is a crying need on another station for someone with her particular experience, and after furlough, she is drafted to a different part of the country? Is this going to create an emotional crisis? Missionaries are supposed to go where they are needed. Is it wise to form an attachment from which it would need an enormous emotional wrench to become detached?

The friendship need not end of course by such a parting of the ways, but it has been known for women to crack up when their 'partner' in the work has been designated elsewhere. Missionary couples will of course always be appointed together. There is no guarantee that this will happen with friends.

What, too, of all the practical considerations—the jointly owned furniture, fitments and car? The splitting up of the home serves to emphasise the severance and can be heartbreaking for the two concerned. However deeply two people may have become intertwined, the needs of other parts of the mission field, or circumstances at home with elderly parents, or health difficulties may necessitate an untwining. There are certain callings which require a particular freedom and availability to be sent anywhere. The missionary calling is one.

Here then is a problem. It is right and good that missionaries should know deeply loving relationships in their work, and love, naturally, will always make us vulnerable. Yet how can they know this love without forming the kind of attachment that makes it difficult for them to be free and available to serve *anywhere* and with *anyone*? Can such people allow themselves to put down deep roots? Roots are necessary, for people who are rootless are rarely able to help others very much. But they need to be roots that are not twined round one person, or one place, or one piece of work. Rather they must be roots that, if pulled up, may bring pain to the individual but do not cause an all-round upheaval. The crux of the problem in the kind of relationship we have been considering, is that two such people begin to find their securities in each other and almost solely in each other. That is the real danger. Our security (if it is truly to be security) must be in God and thereby within ourselves — where God abides.

The second consideration is that of *exclusivism*. I have already touched on this earlier but it deserves further attention. Although it is understandable and right that where two people feel they have a special affinity, they will want to have time to be alone together, nevertheless that mutual love should make them more welcoming and open to others, not less so.

If our two missionary friends are uncertain as to whether or not their relationship has taken a wrong turn, one relevant question to ask is: 'Have we been more hospitable and more outgoing since our love for each other grew? Or have we tended more and more to keep ourselves to ourselves? Are unexpected visitors welcomed or endured?'

Within a Religious Community it would be surprising if monks or nuns did not find themselves more especially drawn to some brothers or sisters than others. At one time particular friendships were discouraged, and indeed feared. Now there is a more realistic acceptance of what is, after all, the human condition. But again, if any Religious is concerned as to the propriety of a relationship, the vital question to ask is: Is our friendship really contributing to the upbuilding and well-being of the Community as a whole? Is it providing just another source of love that wells up to refresh all our sisters and brothers besides ourselves? Does it make us that much more human that we are the more able to live out our religious life? Do we at any time deliberately exclude those in the Community room, or garden, who would love to be drawn into our conversation and into the circle of love? Are we in any sense 'apart' in a selfish way, or has our love for each other so strengthened our loving generally that together we are like a glowing fire to which people are drawn irresistibly to warm themselves?

A third point to remember is that one gift of the single life is *independence*. We should enjoy that *as* a gift, and not squander it or cast it aside lightly. We need to keep some independence not only of spirit but also of our purse strings and our personal agenda. Married people reach their maturity through one avenue (total sharing), while single people on the whole, reach their maturity through another—that of exercising some means of independence. In no way do we express our independence more overtly than in the disposal and use of our time and money.

Consider, for instance, if it is wise to spend all our leisure time with the same friend. If you are sharing a house all the year round, is it a good idea to go away on holiday together too? In some cases it may be the very obvious and right thing to do, but in others there may be good reason to go separate ways, especially if one friend dominates the other, or one leans rather helplessly on the other.

One very sound piece of advice was given us during missionary training by our Principal. 'Keep a private door that you open to no one save God', we were told. However close a friend may be, there needs to be that secret place which is kept for God alone, that closed door which must be shut when we enter His presence, and shut to all other human beings, no matter how dear. Ultimately we must stand alone before God, and it is alone with Him that we need to practise His presence and cultivate our relationship. Some burdens, some griefs, some joys should be kept for His ear alone, if only to remind ourselves that He is 'special' in a way that no human friend can be, and to express in a practical way our dependence upon Him at the very deepest level of our being.

I believe that this is true within marriage as well—even in the matter of prayer. Even for married couples the shared prayer life cannot be a replacement for a personal prayer life with God.

This reminder is most beautifully expressed in a prayer which Temple Gairdner[1] prayed as he prepared for marriage:

> That I may come near to her, draw me nearer to Thee than to her; that I might know her, make me to know Thee more than her; that I may love her with the perfect love of a perfectly whole heart, cause me to love Thee more than her and most of all. Amen. Amen.
>
> That nothing may be between me and her, be Thou between us every moment. That we may be constantly together, *draw us into separate loneliness with Thyself*. And when we meet breast to breast, my God, let it be on Thine own. Amen. Amen.

One may be able to keep the closet door of one's prayer life closed but it may not always be a practical possibility to keep the door of one's bedroom closed. Always keep a separate bedroom however, unless circumstances make it absolutely impossible. In these days of inflation the rent of a flat is often so astronomical it is sometimes an economic necessity to share rooms. A certain measure of privacy is, however, a 'must' for us all.

An ex-student of mine who had enjoyed her single room in

[1] Constance Padwick, *Temple Gairdner of Cairo* (S.P.C.K.), p. 92.

the college hall of residence, went into a flat with two other young teachers. It meant a shared bedroom, shared lounge-cum-study, shared kitchen, shared record player, shared radio, shared larder, etc. She began to find it all a great strain. Laughingly she told me that never before in her life had she taken so many baths, for it was the only place in the flat where she could guarantee privacy. She was lucky. In some flats you can't be sure that even that place will be private!

If a very close friendship develops, it is wise to have separate rooms in order to preserve some necessary 'alone-ness'. This book is about those 'who walk alone'. In some sense we all do, or should, whether we are married or single. Alone-ness is something we need to accept and enjoy. Unless we do so, we cannot grow into full maturity. The greatest danger of an exclusive and very absorbing relationship is not the risk of homosexual practices, but the temptation to throw away all occasions and opportunities for solitude. If we never seek to be alone and come to terms with the real self and grow in our understanding of selfhood, then it cannot be the real self that meets with others. That immediately puts a limit on the depth to which our relationships can go. The discovery of the true self comes through togetherness and alone-ness. He who can be alone and at ease with himself, will be at ease with others. Our emotional development may be stunted if we have no friends, as we have seen, but this is equally true of him who hates solitude.

Let us return to those who cannot have a room alone or any place of privacy or solitude. Such were the circumstances of our Lord Himself, until He could get out on to the hillsides to spend nights alone in prayer. In sharing our humanity, *He* knew what it was to have no privacy. Yet, it was He who said: 'When ye pray, go into your closet and shut the door, and pray in secret . . . ' He had never known what it was to have a room of His own or a 'closet door' to shut, so He must have been referring to that inner sanctum of silence and solitude where one is alone with oneself and God. This is the privacy into which one can retreat whatever the housing conditions; but to be able to open and close the door of that interior room means cultivating the art of detachment.

Wordsworth spoke of 'the bliss of solitude'. It is a bliss all too few people seek. If it is safeguarded, however, particular friendships do not constitute the hazard they might otherwise be.

HOMOSEXUAL FRIENDSHIPS

So far we have been looking at special friendships in which there may be inherent emotional dangers, but which are not necessarily homosexual. The relationship may be between people of the same sex, but the sexual component remains unconscious. Let us be clear and specific however. In any deep relationship there is *always* a sexual element, for we come in friendship as *whole* beings, and that must include the sexual.

One of our problems in any discussion of this sort is that 'sexual' is often confused with what should more accurately be called 'genital'. A relationship may have a very proper sexual component and a very satisfying feeling of complementariness without the least desire for genital expression. It is a different kind of relationship from that which develops between two people who enter into a friendship fully aware that they are both homosexuals and equally aware that as their friendship deepens, there will be the desire to express their love for each other in physical acts. What should we say of these friendships?

Here we are on delicate and sensitive ground. For Christians, this kind of friendship may produce agonising conflicts, as any pastor or confessor will testify.

Let us look at the 'problem' (if that is how it should be termed) from the angle of those who love people of their own sex and, in the sense of looking for partnership, *can only* love in this way.

In these days there is more understanding, enlightenment, openness and sympathy towards such people and for this we ought to be grateful. In *Time for Consent*,[1] Norman Pittenger speaks of some present-day attitudes towards homosexuals. People may be more sympathetic, he claims, but the attitude is still not always right. Some people pity homosexuals, or regard it as a kind of 'sickness'. For the homosexual this attitude is often more hard to accept than outright condemnation.

So far as he can see, he is acting in accordance with his deepest instincts and his most profound impulses; he is behaving according to the 'nature' which somehow has been given him . . . What he is seeking is to give himself to another human being and to receive from another human being the same quality of love as that which he is anxious to give.

To be quite frank I find it difficult not to be indignant at the people who lack understanding of the deepest drives in others but who are quite ready to demand recognition of such drives in themselves. I am indignant at those who can only sneer or condemn, or pity and sigh, or (worst of all, perhaps) laugh indulgently at such 'odd' behaviour and such 'queer' desires. And my indignation can turn to an almost furious attack on those condemning persons, pitying persons, amused persons, asking them if they have no compassion, no fellow-feeling for others, no capacity to grasp the plain fact that everyone is not like themselves.

Nowadays there would probably be few church leaders or theologians who would condemn the homosexual condition as 'sinful'. If a person is so constituted that for him or her, the 'natural' thing is to feel drawn to someone of the same sex, and to long for a deep, loving relationship in which the mutuality is complementary, then this can scarcely be regarded as 'sinful'. St. Paul condemned the *unnatural* vice of those who deliberately cultivated a homosexual relationship in addition

[1] Norman Pittenger, *Time for Consent* (S.C.M.).

to their heterosexual activity.[1] Their natural instincts were heterosexual and for them homosexuality *was* a perversion of natural instincts. This cannot be said of the true homosexual, the man or woman who cannot love in any other way.

Here again we need to beware of the danger of giving labels. All of us have a certain amount of bisexuality in us and there is not as clear a line of demarcation between heterosexual and homosexual as some suppose. Sometimes homosexuals are themselves at fault in insisting on labelling themselves—a fact which only increases their sense of isolation.

There seems to be less agreement over the rightness or wrongness of homosexual acts. Some would say that it cannot be considered sinful to be a homosexual by nature, but it *is* sinful to engage in those acts of tenderness and intimacy which to a heterosexual may seem disgusting or repulsive even though he engages in almost exactly the same love play in his own heterosexual relationships.

In this chapter I would not presume to provide answers. I only seek to raise questions and discuss some current thinking. What we shall consider is a particular attraction between two people who find real fulfilment in their love for each other. We are not here particularly concerned with those who are promiscuous. Promiscuity for homosexuals or heterosexuals is degrading, irresponsible and unsatisfying.

The real, heart-searching questions arise where two people so love each other that they intend to stay together, and to enter into a degree of commitment and mutuality which in a hetero-sexual relationship would inevitably lead to marriage. In recent years some have begun to ask: 'Why should homo-sexuals not have the opportunity of pledging their love for each other before God and their friends, and of promising to remain faithful to one another till "death us do part?" ' Could the church not provide some sort of wedding service for homosexuals?

In the U.S.A. this is already happening in some churches. A

[1] Romans 1:26, 27.

newspaper recently carried the story and photograph of a Baptist minister who had just been 'married' to a young man. We were not told what his congregation felt about this, but the service had been held in his church. In London, two young men asked their vicar for a service of blessing upon their life together. They were just setting up a joint home, and after the service, they threw a little reception-cum-house-warming party, and spoke quite sensibly and openly (not brazenly) of the problems they would have to face in their rather special circumstances.

Where such commitment has been made quite openly it is inevitable that the whole relationship is going to be cemented and sealed in physical acts of love. In these circumstances, is that sinful?

Marriage, in the biblical sense, is intended to give permanence and companionship and make possible procreation. By mutually consenting to enter into an indissoluble union, a man and woman fulfil the aim of permanence. In this union their love grows and deepens through their total trust in each other and gift of themselves to one another. Herein lies the companionship. Their union is a one-flesh union and this is the means of raising a family and fulfilling the procreative function.

If we are to accept the biblical position, does this perhaps give us a guide-line as to whether or not other uses of sex are in fact abuses? As Alex Davidson has pointed out:[1]

Adultery may provide companionship and procreation but not permanence. Fornication would want companionship but not permanence and, one would hope, not procreation. In homosexual practices not only is procreation impossible but permanence is improbable (whatever hopes there are at the outstart, homosexual couples do not usually grow old gracefully together).

[1] Alex Davidson, *The Returns of Love* (I.V.F.).

As was said earlier of particular friendships, however close the friendship, however much the intention of staying together, however many declarations of love are made (even in a public church service), a relationship of this sort is not marriage. It may have many ingredients in common with marriage, but it is not, and never can be, marriage.

Do then the intimacies of married life have a proper and rightful place within such a relationship? Some will undoubtedly answer, 'Yes. What we do as consenting adults to express our love is something entirely between ourselves and our God. We are sure He is in every act of loving and therefore have clear consciences before Him in this matter.'

Others will have gnawing doubts. They may wonder if this is due simply to the conditioning of our society. Had they been Greeks of the first century A.D., would they have had similar compunctions? Or is it not so much a conditioning process as the 'Holy Spirit bearing witness with our spirits that we are the sons of God . . . ?'[1] Since we are more than animal and therefore do not have to be at the mercy of our drives and instincts, can we accept a voluntary self-denial in this area?

No one can blame a homosexual for being so. No one would blame him for having strong sexual desires towards another person; but our desires do not *necessarily* have to be fulfilled. May not the homosexual regard himself as in a similar position to the celibate, or the unmarried heterosexual? If single heterosexual people assume that because they have strong sexual urges, they must satisfy them, they are considered immoral (at least by Christian standards). For heterosexual people to make love outside of marriage is still fornication or adultery—whatever the current laxity. Why should it be thought so much harder for the homosexual to keep his passions under control, and channel those very natural and understandable drives?

Jacques Pasquier[2] has said that to argue this way seems

[1] Romans 8:16.
[2] Jacques Pasquier, 'Celibacy and Effective Maturity'.

plausible at first. 'The fact that homosexuals do appear to have more difficulty in doing so may be due to their relative social isolation (and in some cases a lack of responsible control due to immaturity).'

Is this claim made because there has been more open discussion about the plight of the homosexual, I wonder? Has anyone questioned, for example, those who are physically handicapped—unmarried and unlikely to marry? Their handicap may not have affected or reduced their normal sexual energies at all. Is it not equally hard for them to accept a way of life that excludes normal sexual activity?

What of the mentally handicapped? They may have the mental ages of children and yet be possessed of fully adult sexual urges. Do we say of them, 'They can't help being as they are. Let them express themselves in the only way possible to them'? With their diminished sense of responsibility this could, at times, have appalling consequences. And in all this, are we minimising the difficulty that most ordinary, heterosexual single people have in controlling and channelling *their* sexual instincts and drives?

I wonder very much if the faint hope of a Mr. or Mrs. Right looming up on the distant horizon is all that much of a help when it comes to controlling passions that are behaving like wild horses, that will not be reined in. Even single heterosexual people feel a certain social isolation too. Sometimes homosexuals object that it is harder for them because celibacy is enforced. The heterosexual may accept celibacy voluntarily as the God-given path for him, but a homosexual has no such choice. If this is his objection, he should perhaps think of a lonely, single woman *longing* for friendship with a man, but no one seems particularly interested in her. Has she really got any choice, short of flinging herself at a man? Can we therefore claim that the homosexual state is so entirely different from other forms of singleness? Is it harder for him to contain himself? How does one begin to measure such longings? It is surely not a case of homosexual versus heterosexual. So much depends on the individual degree of sexual energy.

Even if, for argument's sake, we accept that there are exceptional difficulties for the homosexual, it does not follow that he is helpless. When I turn away in abhorrence from a cat playing with a terrified mouse, my friends laugh and tell me; 'It can't help it; it is in its nature.' I may have to learn to accept that of cats, but do I have to accept it of human beings?

Human responsibility implies freedom of choice. For some people the choice is diminished because their freedom is limited, but in all our actions there is *some* element of choice, however small. To say: 'I can't help it', puts us on a level with the animals. It is the cry that went up from Eden and has been echoed by fallen humanity ever since. Maturity implies accepting responsibility.

The Returns of Love[1] is an attempt to show how one homosexual faced the responsibilities of his condition and the renunciation of sexual activity. Christian homosexuals who have tender consciences about physical acts within a loving relationship would do well to consider Alex Davidson's line of approach. Perhaps he points to 'the more excellent way' of love. If those who accept a vow of chastity or celibacy, in one form or another, can still learn to love at great depth without expressing that love sexually, could not the homosexual share that discipline? It is not easy of course, but it is a possible path, for the seat of love is in the will and not the emotions.

For all single, celibate or homosexual Christians the words of the Rule of Taizé[2] may have some application. 'Our "Chastity" means neither a breaking with human affections nor indifference, but calls for the transfiguration of our natural love. Christ alone converts passions into total love for one's neighbour.'

---

[1] Alex Davidson, *The Returns of Love*.
[2] Roger Schutz, *The Rule of Taizé* (The Faith Press), p. 86.

Another point that has to be considered is the element of
selfishness that can be a part of a homosexual relationship.
It is the same danger that applies to all particular friendships
and even to marriage itself, but because of the relative social
isolation that some homosexuals feel, one wonders how far
such friends would be able to be truly outgoing and so to share
their love. Or how far would they be the more turned in
upon themselves? Is the fact that they are unable to share
that love more widely ultimately going to spoil the love
itself?

Perhaps we have been asking the wrong questions about
such relationships. The emphasis seems to have been on
whether or not homosexual acts are morally permissible (and,
until recently, the laws relating to homosexual behaviour
reinforced that attitude), when the primary consideration
should be: 'Is this friendship going to radiate love *out* to others
and draw them *in* to its circle, and share the warmth and joy,
or will it make the partners in the friendship so "apart", so
remote, that they are safe in an ivory tower that effectively
excludes all others?' Every loving relationship should be a
centre of healing and comfort, open and available to all amid
the wounds and sores of society.

These questions must also be asked:

To what extent is this a relationship of mature love (as
opposed to immature infatuation)?

How far is it really promoting my emotional growth and
that of my friend?

Is there any sense in which this could be called a form of
self-indulgence? or inordinate affection?

Has it impaired or deepened my relationship with God? Is
there any element of idolatry in it?

Does it help both of us to become more fully human?

If homosexual friends can, with real honesty, answer these
questions to their entire satisfaction and peace of mind, then
they have nothing to fear. The snag is that we are all such
masters of self-deception and so quick to rationalise our

behaviour that even our selfishness can be given a sugar coating.

I listened once to a discussion with some lesbians who were rationalising behaviour that was blatantly selfish. One question put to them was this: Would they not be sorry that, in a lesbian 'alliance', they would be forfeiting the possibility of children? Two of them said that, of course, they wanted children and were certainly determined to have them—not, let it be added, by adoption. They were calmly contemplating 'using' a man in order to give them children whom they planned to bring up with their female partner. 'I want, therefore I must have' was their attitude. Nothing was said of the child's right to a father as well as a mother. No consideration was given to the feelings of the father—if he had any, or the effect of such an unusual home background on the child. No thought seemed to be given to the morality of the plan. It all smacked more of modern farming techniques and artificial insemination than of responsible human loving. Clearly the maternal instincts will be there in a lesbian relationship, but, again, we need not be slaves to our instincts. The lesbian is in a position no different from any other single woman in her longings for children, but there is the same need for self-control and proper channelling of the maternal drives.

I want to end this chapter on a positive note. It would be well to consider the particular gifts that a homosexual has to offer. Surely we are all meant to enjoy our sexuality, whether we are heterosexual or homosexual. All too often homosexuality is thought of as a blight, a disease, something that needs to be hidden from all but those few who can share at a deep level. Yet it is often the case that the homosexual is a very loving and lovable person with a tremendous contribution to make. He is often far more sensitive and gentle than his heterosexual brother (which is why he is frequently artistic and creative). If he can accept his special gifts as well as his limitations, then he really has an extra quality to offer. For while he may be very masculine and muscular (there is a common misconception that all homosexuals are effeminate), he may also have a great capacity for tenderness and understanding. While tenderness, sensitivity and gentleness are wonderful qualities in whomever they are found, they are especially so in a man. If such gifts are being refined and controlled by the Holy Spirit, then he bears a real Christ-likeness.

The lesbians I heard in the discussion I referred to above, were either rather defensive or simply 'brazening it out' in a public interview, hence the impression of hardness that they gave. But this is not at all typical. Lesbians too are often people of great sensitivity. One such woman told me, with tears streaming down her face, that she had looked upon her condition as a cause of shame and disgust and had prayed earnestly that her 'thorn' should be removed. When it was not removed she then tried to view it as a rather special gift and believed that there would be 'grace sufficient' to accept and use it. I was tremendously impressed by her positivity, and I saw her tears as healthy tears of acceptance rather than self-pity. Her acceptance has released in her a wonderful sensitivity combined with a great strength of character and a loving spirit. She is the 'tower of strength' in any group, and yet people will seek her out to unburden themselves and confide in her because they find in her such patience and deep understanding of human problems.

If people wish to regard homosexuality as a freak of nature, and even if it is not the condition ordained by God when He said that it was not good for man that he should be alone, then we can only rejoice that God is, as ever, bringing good out of evil. We can thus accept with humility the special gifts mediated to us through those who are His homosexual children, our brothers and sisters whom we cannot and would not disown.

CHAPTER FOUR

The Risks of Love—With the Opposite Sex

IN OUR DISCUSSION OF FRIENDSHIP, I SAID THAT THE HEALTHY single person needs a good many friends. If there is to be real richness and variety, this must include friends of the opposite sex. We all *need* friends of both sexes. Just as little boys can enjoy the friendship of little girls in a delightful innocency, so there is a place for innocence in maturity too. Responsible adult men and women can have healthy, happy, deeply satisfying relationships without necessarily contemplating marriage. Men who never mix with women and can count no women amongst their friends are often awkward and ill-at-ease in their presence, and sometimes completely gauche. Equally, women who have no male friends may behave in a very self-conscious way when they meet men, or, alternatively, they may be so paralysed with fear that they present a stony, cold front.

I want in this chapter, to argue for the possibility of learning to love those of the opposite sex and love them deeply without becoming too emotionally knotted-up or sexually involved. Of course there are dangers in such relationships, but this is just another example of the sensible risks that maturity must be prepared to take. After all, there are dangers in driving, but most of us use cars! We shall inevitably make mistakes but so

65

often whole areas of loving have never opened up for some people because they have been too fearful of the risks involved. They are so much the poorer as a result. They love life a little less who have not known love at this kind of level.

Father Bede Jarrett once gave some very good advice to a young monk whose conscience was troubled by the intensity of human love and the fear that it might obscure his spiritual life:

> Then as for the point you mention, I would only say this, that I am exceeding glad. I am glad because I think your temptation has always been towards Puritanism, narrowness, a certain inhumanity . . . You were afraid of life because you wanted to be a saint and because you knew you were an artist . . .
>
> . . . Now evil is overcome by good, by God, by love of God, by reaching for Him everywhere. You must not be afraid of looking for Him in the eyes of a friend. He is there. You can at least be sure of that. To love others is not to lose Him but if possible to find Him in them. He is in them. You will miss finding Him only if you merely love yourself in them. That is the blinding nature of passion; it is self masquerading under a very noble disguise.
>
> I agree that to say that your desire to bring God to Y. is sufficient justification for your friendship is all bunkum . . . You love Y. because you love him, neither more nor less, because he's lovable. You won't find any other sincere reason however hard you try . . . Enjoy your friendship, pay the price of the following pain for it, and remember it in your Mass and let Him be a Third in it. The opening of the Spiritual Fellowship . . . 'Here we are, thou and I, and I hope that between us Christ is a Third'. Oh dear friendship, what a gift of God it is. Speak no ill of it.[1]

We must now turn to some of the problems that can arise, and they are real problems.

In a relationship of deep affection between a single man and a single woman, problems can arise if one of them has a degree of

[1] Evelyn Waugh, *Ronald Knox*, p. 125.

expectation that is different from the others'. Here the need is for utmost honesty and openness. There is the possibility that, if the man's position is not clear, a woman will read more into his actions than he intends. *He* may regard her as a very good friend but *she* may (and probably will, unless there is real understanding) begin to view him as a future husband.

Sometimes women have misunderstood this kind of relationship and have clung to a slim hope for *years* when, in fact, the man had no intention whatever of marrying her.

A man with any real sensitivity would realise what was happening of course and clear the situation up, but sometimes this can be difficult. If he is particularly chivalrous, he will be afraid of upsetting the woman, or he may fear emotional scenes, or he may genuinely fear losing her friendship. So often a kind of cat and mouse game is played out, neither quite knowing how the other feels, with both afraid to say anything that would imply a deeper affection than that which in fact exists.

One result of this kind of confusion is that a woman may cling to such a friendship—possibly with her only man friend—and fail to make other men friends. She may begin to pin all her future hopes on him. The more they are seen around together (especially if never with different partners), the more people will assume there is a tacit understanding between them. Sadly men will sometimes encourage this kind of relationship, not only because they enjoy the companionship, but because it suits their convenience to have a partner for the office dance, or for theatre parties. It can be useful for him to have someone to make up a foursome if he is invited out by a couple. It is flattering to be escorted by an attractively turned out woman. And, perhaps, without realising his own selfishness, he will encourage a girl without regard for the expectations he is building up in her. It is very difficult for a woman who has devoted many years of such close friendship to one particular man, to realise that he is probably incapable of bringing himself to the point of commitment. Some men may get as far as a proposal of marriage and enter into engagement, but at the last minute break it all off because they simply cannot go through with the prospect of anything as lifelong as marriage.

There are obviously a number of psychological reasons for this and it is probably not the intention of such men to hurt their women friends, certainly not to break their hearts. They fail at that point of ultimate commitment just as some people may dive off all the lower diving boards but simply *cannot* bring themselves to take the plunge from the top diving board.

All this can be true in reverse. It could be the woman who is unable to commit herself in the relationship, though it does seem more often to be the other way round. It is a risk, and it can lead to great unhappiness, possibly even, bitterness. The sensible risk must, however, be accompanied by sensible precautions and the first of these is to have more than one such relationship. Other friendships may not mean quite so much, but at least there is more than *one* friendship. It reduces dangerous expectations and it makes it clear to onlookers that it is not a unique and exclusive relationship.

A further point to be considered is this. If one or other in the relationship begins to feel that his or her feelings are going (or have gone) a good deal deeper than those of the other, it would be well to come out with it into the open rather than 'play it cool' without giving any reasons. Hiding feelings will limit the freedom within the relationship and neither will feel the same degree of enjoyment in being together. The woman may, for example, feel desperate and, in her anxiety, decide to tell the man how she feels. If he is at all perceptive he will probably have seen the situation developing and feel thankful to be able to discuss it openly. In that case, he can tell her exactly what his feelings are for her. If they do not include marriage, then she has the choice of ending the friendship (amicably one would hope) or continuing on a different basis. But she knows that she must try and put aside all her particular hopes and learn to love him and enjoy his friendship in an unpossessive and undemanding way.

Either way the decision is painful. The severance of a deep friendship is a form of emotional amputation, with inevitable emotional pain. Fortunately time can heal such wounds and often does, even if the nerves go on tingling for some time. To continue the relationship, having openly declared one's feelings and found an inequality in the kind of loving, is very difficult, and, for many, even impossible. It is a hard path that some have chosen to follow. They need exceptional emotional stamina and discipline, but they share no greater pain than those who, within marriage discover a similar inequality of love and must live more closely to rejection and restraint.

There is another kind of problem that friendships with the opposite sex pose and that is the well-meaning, well-intentioned speculations of other friends. I have heard it said so often: 'There is no such thing as a platonic friendship . . . ' As soon as a woman grows fond of a man, her friends invariably begin to make whispered remarks about 'future possibilities'. When such things are said, it is sometimes possible to laugh them off, but people can be very persistent and are often certain that they know your feelings better than you know them yourself. 'Oh yes, those on the touch-line see so much more of the game than the players' and they nod their heads wisely with that 'we know' look. Yet often they do not know at all, because they cannot know the degree of intimacy or, for that matter, restraint between the friends. In any case, suggestions of marriage are usually embarrassing and unhelpful. They may even create hopes where there were not any, or they may make it necessary to be extremely guarded and, regretfully, even secretive about what one reveals of a particular friendship. It is a pity to have to be guarded where one could be open. You may even worry that if this is what one's own friends are saying, what is being said to the other 'party'? And confusion becomes worse confounded.

This leads me to yet another problem—that of scandal. Those

who cannot understand a deeply loving relationship between two single people who intend to remain single, may suppose that there is something questionable about such a friendship. They imagine that here are two people who are probably enjoying all the privileges and pleasures of marriage without accepting its responsibilities. So they begin to make comments like: 'It's very odd that those two haven't married, isn't it? They frequently spend time together and are obviously very fond of each other. You're not going to tell me that they are that friendly and sometimes alone and *still* only just friends.' Before anyone can stop it, suspicions mount and rumours grow.

It is a sad fact that people sometimes have to curtail a relationship, not because they fear each other in any way, but because they fear possible gossip, in which neither would want to involve the other.

I do plead that other friends leave single people to enjoy friendships between the sexes without speculating, gossiping, interfering or commenting. Allow relationships to take their own course, and deepen of their own accord. Rejoice, encourage and, if asked, advise, but never try to manipulate the lives of others. This can be a dangerous game to play and, in any case, it is really the prerogative of Almighty God, Who *alone* can 'order the unruly wills and affections of sinful men'.[1]

In spite of the risks which I have spelled out, the need for single people to have friends of the opposite sex is still there and should not be frustrated nor repressed. A man needs a woman's tenderness and trust and a woman needs the courtesies, honour and respect a man can give as well as the warmth of an embrace. Fortunately in these days there is a great deal more freedom to love, and love openly, than our Victorian predecessors knew but, while permissiveness is growing apace, we are only on the threshold of true freedom in this realm.

There should be a greater openness particularly within the

[1] Collect for the Fourth Sunday after Easter.

Church, the Body of Christ. It has started to happen—for which we can be grateful to God. One outcome of the charismatic renewal is a more overtly warm relationship between people of the opposite sex as well as of the same sex. Men and women can kiss each other warmly without impropriety. It is an expression of genuine affection and of brotherly and sisterly love at its highest human level. Sisters of one religious community will greet 'with a holy kiss' brothers of another. How right that they should feel able to do so. In some churches when the Pax is given within the communion service, it is a *kiss* of peace—not merely a folding of each one's hands over another's.

One of the loveliest scenes in *Godspell* (a musical on the life of Christ which hit the West End of London in 1972) seemed to me to be Jesus' farewell to His disciples, where each disciple in turn was given a special personal gesture and each was embraced with obvious warmth and love (men and women alike) which was deeply moving. How much more so when it is the real thing between those who are His present-day disciples! I have attended communion services where, at the end, all have embraced each other very warmly without let or hindrance. Somehow it has seemed fitting, right, healthy and holy. There has not been a hint of 'sexiness' or impropriety anywhere. May such openness and freedom increase within the Body of Christ and be a witness and a sign to our permissive age that true love can express itself without lust.

Some who read this may be wondering how such deeply loving relationships between men and women begin to develop, and what opportunities there are for finding friendship that reaches that level. One of the most obvious ways is through some mutual interest, or through working jointly on a particular project. It may be running a youth club or a charity organisation. It may be working together in the field of drama or music or politics, where there are many shared experiences, shared nervous tensions and shared joy, shared travelling and shared celebrations. It may be some creative work such as a design project or mural or the joint writing of a book. One person went so far as to argue that both sexes are needed, not simply in the act of procreation but for *all* acts of creation.

Such a coming together in order to create must inevitably bring special bonds and goes a long way towards complementarity. A man and a woman will bring out in each other qualities that are not brought out by those of their own sex. This can certainly be seen, for instance, in discussion where male and female will spark each other off in a way not experienced in all-male or all-female conversation.

This is true, also, of leadership, especially within the Church. The happiest combination seems to be the bringing together of the male ability to organise, direct and think objectively, with the female gift of intuition, perception and practical common sense. The result is a thoroughly good bit of team work. It is because women have such a distinctive role to play in Church life, using their *particular* gifts to complement those of men, that it is sad to discover any spirit of competition. The Women's Lib. Movement may be making some right emphases, but I cannot help feeling that it is overlooking to a marked degree the exciting (and liberating!) role that woman has, of complementing man rather than competing with him.

Some people form friendships through their colleague-ship, for example, within a mixed staff room or senior common room. This may be particularly so if they are involved in work on a joint undertaking. There is the colleague-ship of a team ministry where ministers, parish workers, secretaries, and others work closely together. Similar friendships are often formed within an office or club, or within church circles.

One warning note should be sounded however. A friendship may spring up while people are working together on a common project but when the particular project is completed, the nature of the friendship may alter. The glue that kept the relationship together was mainly the work. When that glue has melted away, the two friends may find that they are not nearly so close. They will continue to be friends but not in quite the same way. This may constitute a threat to one or other or both of them and they may sense a certain rejection or cooling off.

This is only a warning, for more often than not two such people who have initially formed a friendship because of a common task, will soon see beyond the work to each other and learn to love and respect each other for themselves alone. The work then becomes for them simply their medium of introduction. Not all single people are lucky enough to be involved in such a working relationship with another single person of the opposite sex. Either they are of the same sex or one of them is married. If close bonds then grow, there are particular difficulties and dangers which are considered elsewhere in this book.

Sometimes a woman will feel a great bond with those men whom she comes to know and trust in their professional capacity and who, in that capacity, can rightly and properly discuss personal matters with her, and show a degree of tenderness. (For a moment, let us discuss the situation from the woman's point of view, though doubtless there is a male counterpart to each female problem.) I refer to such people as her lawyer, her boss, her doctor, her minister or priest. Someone once remarked that for some women these are the only men in their lives. It is true that for some, there are few opportunities to talk to men, let alone make friendships. It is not altogether surprising then that where a discussion with a lawyer, doctor or minister comes as a welcome change from female chatter, a woman may be tempted to engineer appointments with them. It is not always done consciously, but the longing to have the undivided attention of a man, albeit over some quite minor matter, is met by seeking their help.

Do not judge a woman too harshly for this. A more positive step would be to introduce her to other men with whom she might form friendships.

The minister is probably in the most vulnerable position of all those I have mentioned, for although the doctor may be the family doctor and know her well, although the lawyer may be most friendly and helpful, having known her family for years, both of them will keep a certain aloofness, mindful that business is business and that they are employed for their professional expertise. Both are surrounded by fairly solid protections — fixed hours or surgeries, separate home and office telephones, secretaries who can act as intermediaries if necessary. Neither will be willing to give unlimited time to one patient or client. But the parson has far more difficulty in setting bounds and guarding his privacy. He must be a friend and help to everyone, available to all in real need. This is his calling and he accepts it gladly (for the most part) but some people are quite shameless in the demands they make on him. In moments when he feels trapped by a demanding relationship, he may well want to sing, 'Preserve me from my calling's snare'!

Since it is not altogether an uncommon problem in the ministry — to find people forming strong and particular attachments for the minister or priest, it may be worthwhile pausing to consider it briefly.

What most women need and long for in men are not so much sexual relations, not passion, but tenderness and understanding (though naturally one would hope that sexual activity would include great tenderness and sometimes passion). Because most ministers or priests will show understanding and gentleness when anyone is confiding problems to them, it is all too easy for a woman to get emotionally confused. What she longs for in friendship is being given to her generously and honourably so, if she finds it nowhere else, can one wonder that she will cling to that and want more of it? Sometimes she may even get her lines crossed and confuse her love for God with her love for the one who mediates to her the grace of God. This at times can lead to confusion between His will and his will! All ministers and priests experience at some time the problem of those (not always women) who become too emotionally attached to them. 'Every church has one,' I've heard it said rather cynically.

How does one realise the point at which, all unwittingly,

love has become fixed on the channel rather than on God Himself? Worse still, how does one help another to see their own confusion in such a situation? It is so right and natural that people should develop a genuine love for those who share with them their spiritual battles and burdens. The very tenderness that the confidant shows is likely to foster a deeper growth of that love. But it is a love that has emotional risks and will need constantly to be purified and kept on course lest it become a burden or snare to both concerned.

Clearly, all that has been said here of the emotional dangers in this kind of relationship can apply to men as well as women. It is more difficult to recognise the symptoms where men are concerned and therefore more difficult to get disentangled. The danger may also come from the priest's side. He can be emotionally involved in a wrong way. His masculine sexuality may come out in a domineering or possessive way.

Perhaps this shows up a deficiency in practice within many of our churches. The pastoral responsibility has all too often been left to the minister alone. Sometimes this is the fault of the minister who wants to keep everything within his grasp. More often it is the fault of the laity who will be satisfied with no help other than that which the minister can give. It is clear from the New Testament that, in the early church, the 'caring for the flock' was the responsibility of the elders as well as priests. It should be so now. Every church has more than one man (or woman) of God. We often put far too much strain on our clergy by assuming that they are the only ones who can give counsel and advice, so it is partly this kind of thinking that is responsible for the wrongful emotional attachments we have been considering here. It is a further indication that within the 'Body' all gifts must be used and valued so that it is a genuine team ministry. In a really loving community, as the church should be, those who are crying out for affection and personal caring ought to be able to find it within a group, and not have to leave everything to the minister.

One of the most encouraging signs in some of the churches that are presently experiencing renewal is the new love that is being fostered between members. This is the real hall-mark of the work of the Holy Spirit, for the loving is such that it envelops all who come within its orbit. And the caring is not reserved for Sundays alone but extends throughout the week to every area of need. There is a real network of shared prayer requests, immediate visits to the sick, practical help for those moving in or moving out of the district, hospitality for those in need of it, and a host of little ministries that all spell LOVE IN ACTION. There need be few qualms for those who 'walk alone' in a group such as this.

Does this suggest an area of lay training that has been sadly neglected in the past? It is not unusual for a church to run teach-ins on prayer, courses on lay evangelism, or systematic Bible study. But has there been enough training in caring, the simple and practical ways in which love can really be expressed? As children we had to be trained to open doors for people, help them across the road, pick up things they had dropped and return them, etc. It was training that produced awareness. Similarly in our church life, in more important and adult circumstances, the lack of caring is often due, not to un-willingness to help, but sheer ignorance of the needs of others and how to set about meeting them. A measure of practical organisation in this field of service could be of immense help, especially if it were backed by sound biblical teaching. In this way false notions of the practical versus the spiritual or the sacred versus the secular would not be encouraged, and people would see Christian love being expressed in its totality. Training in awareness can be only a small part of this caring. The mainspring will be the love of God Himself which is always overflowing and must find channels of expression.

JESUS AND RELATIONSHIPS

What problems did our Lord face in this whole realm of

personal relationships? To look at this question may give real help to some of us.

The Gospel records show that Jesus had a number of women friends, women who loved him deeply and whom he loved in return. They loved him for what he was. They loved him too because of his acceptance of them, no matter what their past had been. His courtesy and his tenderness called out the true womanhood in them and helped them to be the selves they most longed to be. But the gain was not just on one side. Women clearly ministered to his need also.

In thinking along these lines we can see not only the needs of Jesus himself but those of single men as a whole and perhaps especially those engaged in the ministry of the Church. Perhaps here we can argue from the particular to the general. Our Lord, for example, *needed conversation with women* (in that he was fully human, and full humanity implies the need of relationships with both sexes). It was not that he put up with it when courtesy so demanded. He enjoyed talking with them. He revelled in the quick repartee of the Syrophoenician woman.[1] Mary ministered to his needs far more effectively than Martha, with all her bustling in the kitchen in the certainty that his hunger must be his uppermost need. She realised how much he wanted to sit and talk at a deeper level. He obviously enjoyed *being in a home* and, at the right times, he certainly would have appreciated Martha's hot, nourishing meals. He was probably very grateful to her for other acts of love. Did she occasionally do some washing for him? He must have been a wonderful guest. Any little service rendered would be outweighed by the pure joy of having him about the house. Peter's mother-in-law would have delighted to minister to him and possibly he, in turn, would have been soothed and comforted by a little occasional 'spoiling'. How often, one wonders, would he have taken refuge at the house of Mary (Mark's mother)? Must it not have been good to get away, at times, from the constant companionship and occasional quarrelling of men?

[1] Mark 7:26.

Our Lord was not *afraid* to venture into relationships with women—though there were obvious risks involved. In a culture where marriages were usually arranged rather than left to the dictates of the heart, perhaps there was less danger of women falling in love with him, but there still must have been the risk of their growing to love him in the wrong way. After all, he was the 'Proper Man', and they would have discovered in him all the very best of manhood—a fine physique, a good mind, immense physical strength, great gentleness, understanding, pure love and a wonderful sense of humour. It would have been surprising if women had not loved him. We know that his critics accused him of being the friend of prostitutes and sinners because his deep compassion and understanding of human nature, together with the divine love that flowed in and through him, led him to accept, and even welcome them, as of infinite worth. And his reverence for their womanhood made them see themselves in a new light. With that new self-respect came hope.

Even so, the response to that love must have been varied. Fortunately some light is shed on them in the Gospels. It would have been so easy for women who loved him, in the first place out of deep gratitude, to have followed him around like devoted little dogs, trying in every way to please him. Yet what he needed was their mature friendship, not simply their devotion. It would have been a revolutionary concept in the Jewish world of that day—though the Greeks were familiar with such friendships between men and women. The 'hetairai' (the cultured mistresses of famous men) played a very distinctive and important part in the life and thought of ancient Greece. The needs which Jesus felt are, in a way, a pattern of the needs felt by those who as bachelors or celibates, minister within his Body. They need the mature friendship of women that will challenge their own growth.

Sometimes women smother a single man with a kind of 'mother hen' activity, so concerning themselves with the matter of his washing, the cleaning of his house, looking after him when he is ill, that, all unwittingly perhaps, they are treating him as a little boy rather than as a fully adult man. Of course, there are practical necessities, and a man on his own will sometimes be very grateful for help with his meals and laundry but, on the whole, he won't want pampering. Perhaps women should ask themselves first before offering help: 'Why am I doing this? Is it primarily out of concern for my friend or are maternal instincts taking over?'

Some bachelors are quite happy to go on being mothered in every possible way, but women should beware of pandering to *that* too. They are not helping towards maturity if they do. It seems to be ingrained in our thinking that men are not nearly as capable as women in respect of looking after themselves. We do not expect them to be good home-makers, yet in fact, many bachelors run their homes smoothly and efficiently. They decorate them more tastefully than many women would. They cook superbly and economically and no visitor to their home would be aware of excessive dust or squalor. The kichen is not piled high with a week's dirty crocks, nor do they appear in grubby shirts or socks with holes. If single men are capable of looking after themselves (as many of them are) and it is not going to mean a curtailment of other essential work, then let them do it. Don't try and persuade them otherwise by waiting on them hand and foot.

As opposed to the temptation to 'mother' where mothering is not needed, there is the temptation to adopt the role of the devoted but over-dependent child. Especially is this true where relationships with men in the ministry are concerned. There are women who must run to 'Father' or 'Pastor' with every trifling little problem. Having found him sympathetic, understanding and loving in the first instance, they plague him till he is weary of their constant approaches, to ask his advice about things they *ought* to decide for themselves. Here it is not the woman who wants to be the mother, rather she wants to keep the parson in a father-role (and this does not apply only to single priests either).

There is, of course, a proper place for dependence but it is far more likely to lead to a mature relationship if it is inter-dependence. Perhaps it would be true to say that in friendship between any single people of the opposite sex the woman should *vary* her role. Sometimes she will need to be a mother, a sister, a child, or just an adult. Similarly the man will at times find himself in the role of father, or brother, or child, as well as friend. They are not necessarily left deeply unsatisfied because the one role that is not open to them is that of husband or wife.

Turning to a very practical question in our consideration of relationships with the opposite sex, we must now ask how love may be expressed unashamedly in such a friendship without embarrassment or misunderstanding?

Only a prude would object to a kiss, provided it was chaste rather than passionate. A friendly hug is not necessarily going to send the blood pressure up or set all the wrong wheels in motion. There would be times when it would be right to take a hand or arm in courtesy or sympathy—or simply *as* an affirmation of friendship. One should not need to fear *all* bodily contact. It has been said that Christians have been too ready to take out of context the 'Touch me not' of Jesus and apply it to all situations. Love sometimes needs to express itself through touch as much as through words and gifts. Our Lord himself recognised this need when he touched the eyes of the blind man, when he touched the lepers, when he laid his hands in blessing on the children. In all these cases, words alone *could* have been enough.

One of the greatest expressions of love is, of course, the gift of time. To give time to a friend and give it generously is an obvious way of telling him that you love him and you want to be with him, that you enjoy his company, that you delight to share his news and yours with him. If when friends come together, they know that they haven't got to cover a wide range of matters in a very short space of time but have long enough to be truly leisurely, they can relax into a companionable silence. Just being together, without feeling uncomfortable if neither wants to talk, is one of the surest ways of deepening a friendship.

Friendship grows, too, by sharing the fruits of one's thinking. Perhaps the reason why some promising relationships never blossom is that the level of conversation is always superficial, even to the point that friends never really grow to know each other's minds and what they feel about the deeper things of life. A friendship can pall if there are no times when two people can be completely serious.

So then love can be expressed through touch, time and thought (for a start). It is good in such a friendship to share a variety of experiences. If two people only meet at the club, at work or at church, then they only get to know one side of the other. Friends need to share fun and laughter, serious conversation and perhaps even argument. They need to see each other at work and at leisure, at home and at a social gathering, alone and in company, dressed up for special occasions and in casual wear.

In fact, some of the things that apply in courtship, apply in this sort of relationship too. The difference of course lies in the fact that the friends are aware that it is not leading to marriage, and they accept that both have the right (perhaps even the duty) to have the same level of friendship with other people without any sense of disloyalty and, one would hope, without giving rise to jealousy.

All this adds up to the risk of loving. We must never underestimate the difficulties, nevertheless there is a risk which, if taken responsibly, can bring such fun, joy and deep fulfilment. No one should seriously fear to take it.

6

CHAPTER FIVE

The Risks of Love—in the Triangular Relationship

THERE IS AN ASPECT OF FRIENDSHIP WHICH NEEDS TO BE LOOKED at honestly and realistically. It is a risk in loving that is fraught with difficulties and dangers and it is a path on which many have stumbled. Yet, if the dangers can be avoided and one can pick one's way over the stumbling-blocks, the experience is an enriching one. I refer, of course, to friendship between single people and married people.

This area of relationships needs to be looked at in two ways. Firstly there is the friendship of a single person with a married couple and then secondly there is the friendship of a single person with one partner of that marriage.

Most married couples have their single friends. In most cases they would probably speak warmly and enthusiastically of the value they place on such friendships. Often the single person, who happens to live fairly near, is on sufficiently close terms to be able to drop in quite frequently. Perhaps those who are married are not always aware how much single people love to relax in the atmosphere of a home and within a family. It is a situation so different from the average bachelor flat or bed-sitter. Perhaps the couple do not always realise just what it is they are sharing with their single friends. For them family life has become commonplace and they have forgotten some of those aspects of emptiness that can be part of singleness. It is not however usual for the giving to be all on one side. The single person has an important contribution to make too and often brings the breath of a somewhat different world into the friendship. Wives who have to spend much of their time at home with young children are often particularly appreciative of this. 'Married women who respect their single friends for what they are, tell us that they value visits from them to relieve their own loneliness and to prevent them from becoming stale.'[1] Friendship with a single working woman can give a wife a window on to that outside world of the office, the shop, or the school that was once her world, and can help her to feel 'in touch'. When single women begin to feel uneasy or even guilty about the depth of their friendship with wives, they need to remind themselves (having assured themselves that there is no real justification for their guilt) that a married woman often needs the friendship of a single woman as much as the other way round.

For the wife who is perpetually tired and has little freedom or time to find out what is going on in the outside world feels that she is not an interesting companion for her husband. The single woman's hardship is that she is not particularly close to anyone, but she meets many people, and this enables her to communicate with her married friends, with their depth of experience, so that both are enriched.[2]

Difficulties may arise in this kind of friendship if a single person becomes so friendly with a married couple and their children that he or she becomes too much one of the family. It is lovely to know the closeness of being 'family'. It is good to be welcomed, accepted and trusted, and single people in such a favoured position are blessed indeed. It is marvellous for all concerned when the single friend can drop in without any

[1] *The Single Woman*, ed. Elizabeth Mitting (Victory Press), p. 74.
[2] Ibid., p. 74.

special fuss being made, when he or she accepts the family *just as it is* without criticism or comparison, fitting in easily with them, enjoying a romp with the children, helping with the chores and relaxing in front of the fire.

Many who have opened their homes in this way would agree that the pleasure has been mutual. Single friends often have much to give, and can be thoroughly fun loving and full of enthusiasm.

One outstanding example of this was the case of the missionaries Douglas Thornton and Temple Gairdner of Cairo. The two men were working in close harness as bachelor missionaries and when Thornton married, he and his new wife invited their single friend to share their tiny apartment. Gairdner accepted.

'If I *may* live with you and your Elaine, I only hope that I shall not spoil your newly-wedded bliss. Remember that two is company, three is none. So the world would say; perhaps you, she and I know better, "where two or *three*. . ." '

The event proved the world wrong and the experiment an unqualified success. 'My almost brother and sister here,' Gairdner called his host and hostess, and Mrs. Thornton said: 'No one less delicate than Temple could have lived with newly married people, but he was a joy to both of us.'[1]

This was certainly a most unusual experiment, but then the circumstances of their missionary life were unusual too. Normally speaking it would be anything but ideal for a newly married couple to have a close friend as a lodger, but this succeeded because of one thing. Mrs. Thornton hit upon it when she said 'No one less *delicate* than Temple . . .'

One of the reasons why married people may hesitate to open their homes to a single person is simply that not all single people show such delicacy. Sometimes married people have found that, in opening their door a little, it has been pushed wide open by their single guest. Because it is opened once or twice, it is assumed that it will be open at all times. What pleasure there

[1] Constance Padwick, *Temple Gairdner of Cairo*, p. 74.

THE RISKS OF LOVE—TRIANGULAR RELATIONSHIP 85

was at first for the married couple slowly turns to irritation and, maybe, pent up fury. True delicacy will allow *them* the joy of taking the initiative.

Delicacy and tact are needed for single people who *live* with married friends but there may be problems, too, even when the single person is not actually living in the same house. If, for example, he or she is in a lonely bed sit and knows that round the corner there is fun and laughter, warmth and hospitality together with an open invitation to 'come whenever you like—don't sit in that lonely room by yourself', is it to be wondered at that he or she will be strongly drawn to drop in often? Only the very firmly disciplined and unselfish will be able to resist the temptation to call, perhaps *every* time they feel lonely.

How many single people have to look back with bitter regrets and acknowledge the ways in which gradually (for it *is* gradual) they came to abuse their privileges in this respect. Their own needs were often uppermost in their minds and it was easy, in those moments of choice, to rationalise the situation and find excuses for turning up (to help with the ironing, to ask advice, to share some news) insensitive to the groans of the family at yet another appearance! Some such relationships between single people and families work out very well and the friend-ship remains life-long. The single friends may be closer than any aunt, uncle or cousin, possibly closer by the very fact that they are *not* relatives. At other times such friendships have become a burden rather than a delight and have ended disastrously. Few of us have survived single life without making some errors of judgment in this area of relationships. Because it happens often, it is worth drawing attention to it in our consideration of the problems of those who walk alone.

The first thing to be said is this. Mistakes may be avoided and friendships deepened rather than destroyed if there is, above all, a proper selflessness and sensitivity. A single person (and here I shall use the feminine pronoun since men are less involved in this way) needs to guard against becoming selfishly involved with a married couple. For example, while accepting that their invitations as genuine, she must limit the number of her visits to ensure that the couple have enough time alone and with other friends. She must keep an open heart for others who welcome friendship as well as this one special family. She needs to learn to enjoy solitude so that her happiness is not entirely dependent upon having company or being in company. Courtesy, thoughtfulness, commonsense, independence and selflessness are all necessary.

The married couple must be careful too. Be judicious as to *how* invitations are extended. If you say to a single person, 'You *know* you are welcome at any time' and if you press invitations upon them to join you on *every* family outing, *every* weekend, *every* party or special celebration, you must not be surprised if they begin to take it for granted that they will be invited! They have a right to take you at your word and sometimes a married couple have made an enormous fuss of a single friend, urged him or her to share their family occasions, obviously enjoyed their friendship and the company and then, suddenly, have realised that they were no longer free to control the situation. Instead of the *fun* of inviting the friend, it is now *expected* of them. Instead of the keen anticipation of their company, it becomes a duty. They have ended up with more than they bargained for, literally an adult addition to the family. Gradually the relationships begins to turn sour and the married couple feel trapped, all because they were unwisely reckless at the start.

It is tricky when this happens. Some solve it by 'blowing hot and cold' in their attitude, being wildly friendly at times and almost hostile at others. This is certainly not the right answer, for it is both unloving and rude. None of us likes to be tossed to and fro like a cork on the tides of other people's affections. If the single person is courageous enough to face up to what is happening, she may drop the whole relationship, but it is not always that simple. The close involvement with her married friends may mean that she has neglected other friendships and a parting of this sort would mean a terrible emptiness. She may not have the courage to step into that void voluntarily, so she dithers on the edge, hoping that she will not be pushed into it. If you tire of a car you can change it. You can move house if the one you have does not suit you. But you cannot 'change' friends in the same way. You cannot play around with human affections. Emotional ties have been made and it is impossible to sever them painlessly. The children may have become very attached to the single friend and they would be puzzled and hurt should the visits stop.

Those who have known a deep friendship that began with gay abandon and ended with a closed door know the pain, humiliation, and sense of loss this can bring. There is more than one kind of bereavement in this life. The abrupt ending of a friendship can cause just as much heartache and can leave as large a gap in life as the physical death of a loved one. The difference in this 'death' is that the pain is too often borne alone. Some who have suffered in this way will carry emotional scars to the grave. For others, there are open wounds that will not heal . . . and wounds that don't heal tend to fester. Many neuroses and mental illnesses are due to unconscious resentment and to unhealed memories. We should not, of course, create situations where such painful experiences occur. But they do happen. How can we deal with painful memories of past mistakes? How do we rid ourselves of the guilt of having behaved selfishly and wrongly, and in a way that has brought hurt to others?

The story is told of James Craik, a schoolteacher in the Midlands, who was remembered by his pupils because, when they gave in their work to be marked often spoiled by ugly blots, he would sometimes take his pen and doodle round the blots till he had turned them into pictures of angels.

We all need the power to turn our blots into angels. Of course what we would *really* like is the ink eradicator, but it is only transformation that is possible.

BLOTS INTO ANGELS

How do we transform the blots into angels? Since we cannot forget painful memories, how do we deal with them?

I know of no more healing way than through an honest facing of oneself, without shrinking from the truth. It may help too if we can find the courage to put our shame into words in the presence of a trusted friend or adviser, and then either with our friend or alone, bring it to God. We do this not in terms of self-hatred, but in true sorrow for the past. In doing this we experience the reality of forgiveness and the joy and release that go with it.

Forgiveness does not root out painful memories but allows us to use them positively. We can gain a deeper sensitivity and understanding of the pain of others. But this can happen only when we have honestly faced these past failures and confessed them to God, not only because we need peace of mind but because we really do see them for what they are, ugly black blots. Confession that springs from real sorrow is liberating. We no longer feel the bondage of our past failures.

Deep down we all long to be accepted. When we come to God with our failures, we can be *assured* that we are accepted by Him. Often we experience this assurance more fully when we take the costly step of sharing our shame with another person. When we find ourselves freely accepted in love and understanding by *them*, it helps to reinforce God's acceptance of us in our own minds. What can separate us from the love of God? As St. Paul says, 'I am persuaded that nothing can separate us, neither things present' nor things past, he might well have added.

One thing that emerges clearly throughout our consideration of personal relationships is the need for the utmost honesty and integrity in them. Healthy relationships require the courage to be open and straightforward, not in any blunt or clumsy way but in the true sensitivity of love. For example, married people must not issue magnificently generous invitations which are not sincerely meant (and they need to think ahead to the future and not be carried away at the beginning by the novelty of a friendship). If, however, their invitations *are* genuine but have been misunderstood and abused, then they will need to say something by way of guidance to their single friend before things get to such a pitch that it is too late. Similarly single people will need to be really honest about their needs, both with themselves and with their married friends. Do they find themselves wondering:

Am I making a nuisance of myself?

Should I accept every invitation, or would it be kinder to decline some, not because I wouldn't love to accept but in order to protect my married friends from being over generous in their sharing?

Do either of the partners feel any irritation or resentment, however slight, at my frequent visits?

Am I subconsciously persuading myself that they need me when the truth is that I am governed by my need of them?

Are there any ways in which I am spoiling the friendship?

If so, then it would be as well to thrash the matter out with the couple concerned. Of course it would not be altogether easy to open up in such a way as to tell them truthfully that there are these fears and niggling doubts lurking around, but most married couples would respect so honest an appraisal even if it meant dragging out a few painful home-truths which would be as hard to give as to receive. Small doses of pain at that stage are infinitely easier to bear than the pain of not knowing where one stands. It is better to clear the air when the atmosphere seems strained than leave things till they necessitate a total estrangement. Maybe the single person will be relieved through such an openness to discover that the niggles and doubts have not been bothering the married friends at all, that there is really nothing to worry about. The married friends would probably still appreciate the thoughtfulness that prompted the question.

It is not always the single friend who may be guilty of selfishness. There can be faults on both sides. It is possible for a married couple to become wrongly dependent upon the companionship of a single person, and become possessive of him or her. They may come to *expect* frequent and regular visits to their home. They may take it for granted that they should be put in the picture about the movements and affairs of their single friend. Mostly this would be the wish of the single person too but, on both sides, when freedom goes out of the sharing, much of the delight goes too.

There is another angle on all this. Couples should remember that they have a distinct advantage over single people in any relationship. They have each other. It is unlikely therefore that they will ever place as much importance on the friendship as their single friend does. It means that there can be a slight imbalance in the relationship which may make for insecurity where the single person is concerned. Usually there is mutual entertainment in each other's homes but because it is often easier for one to make a journey rather than a whole family, or because it is easier to make room for one more in the family circle than for four or five to descend upon a bachelor flat, it is likely that the single person will be the guest of her friends more often than their hostess. This too can sometimes provoke worry, because there appears to be an inequality in giving.

It may help married people to understand their single friends better if they realise that deep down there may be these fears—the fear of being expected as a frequent visitor, or resented as an intruder; the fear of being accepted simply for their usefulness rather than for themselves alone. This fear is fed if it is clear to the single person that he/she is only invited when a baby-sitter is needed, or another car is required for transport, or an extra person wanted to make up the right number for a party. All friends would want to help in these ways of course, provided that they were not the *only* occasions on which their company was sought.

More often than not married people do consider single

people's needs in a very generous way. You can almost hear
them saying:

'Wouldn't it be a good idea to invite so-and-so round today?
It's her third weekend on her own.'

or, 'He has just had a run of misfortune at work and will be
feeling a bit low,'

or, 'She has had a row, she'll need to talk.'

'There's a specially good T.V. programme that he would
enjoy. We *must* ask him round.'

'He has not been too well and has been cooped up alone for
several days. Wouldn't it be good for him to have a change of
scenery?'

I once had the privilege of living with a family where scarcely
a day went by without conversation such as this taking place
over the breakfast table or at night round the fire. Both
husband and wife had big open hearts that went out to any
who were lonely, needy, sad or afflicted in any way. As well as
their own three children, they had a huge closely-knit family
circle and kept in touch with them all. Their home and car
were at the disposal of their church members in a wholly
generous way. A steady stream of visitors poured in and out of
their home throughout their married life and, while they have
never been rich in terms of this world's goods, they are nevertheless rich. They have loved much and they are much loved
in return. To me that home will always be the example, *par
excellence*, of the joy and enrichment that openness can bring.
In a recent presidential address[1] the husband took as his theme
'Our business is persons', and his speech was entirely consistent
with the lifelong concern he and his wife have shown for
others.

Yet another aspect of the triangular relationship relates to
the friendship of a single woman with the wife and a single
man with the husband in a partnership. It is possible to demand
too much emotionally from one member of a family and care

[1] Presidential Address given at the Baptist Union Assembly, April 30th, 1973.

must be taken not to indulge selfishly in this respect. The single woman who wants to claim the wife as a 'bosom pal' is going to put too great a strain on her when she has loyalties to her husband and children. She simply hasn't the energy or freedom to give herself in such a way, and that kind of attachment can be a real bone of contention between her husband and herself. Of course the wife will want her women friends but her availability cannot be that of, for example, another single woman. Her desire to give as much as possible in friendship to a single friend could set up real tensions in her if that giving in any way conflicted with her family responsibilities. If single people can suffer from fears and guilt that swirl around below the surface of the conscious, married people can be equally affected.

A single man can be a great companion to the husband, but he needs to guard against luring him away from his wife on every possible occasion when he is not working. Of course a young man likes to be free to 'go off with the lads' and to revert to his bachelor days of freedom. Many sensible wives accept that their husbands enjoy an evening out with their men friends and are happy for them to go, but it is a different matter if she is expected to stay at home with the children *every* Saturday afternoon while her husband rushes off with his pals to watch a football match. She will probably encourage him to have an evening out at a club with his friends, but inevitably there has to be a limit to such regular commitments, and a bachelor friend needs to remember that his married friend is not as free as he is, either with his time or his money. In kindness a single friend should be careful not to put undue temptation in the married man's way or flaunt his freedom in this respect in his friend's face. Naturally a man does not like to appear mean in front of his friends and in true generosity he may spend far more than he can afford during an evening out. Only later does he come down to earth with a bump as he remembers family expenses that have to be met. A single man should then protect his married friend from embarrassing situations where he is likely to end up in financial difficulties. He needs to be careful how he speaks of his expensive hobbies or holidays, just as the single woman must exercise tact when talking of her latest buy in clothes and personal effects when chatting to her married friend who is struggling on a lean house-keeping allowance.

All married couples will be glad of baby-sitters from time to time and will love their single friends for offering to look after the children for a day or a weekend to allow them to have a break. There is a danger, however, of single people encouraging or claiming too much affection from the children. Usually the affection grows naturally and in a totally unselfconscious way on both sides, and it is entirely right that children should express their love warmly and unreservedly. But it would be wrong for the single friend to monopolise them in any way, or to draw them away (however unintentionally) from their parents too often, causing even a moment's heartache.

Sometimes it happens that the children find it easier to unburden themselves to the single friend than to one or other of the parents. While this might cause hurt, a wise parent will learn to accept it, remembering that, as children, it was not always to *our* parents that we turned for advice. It may be that the single person is sometimes asked to act as a go-between and is sometimes asked for advice and support in a way that would subtly cause him to 'take sides'. Single people need to be wary of this. While it is right to have the confidence of children, it would be very wrong to contradict the wishes of the parents at any point and so create a conflict of loyalties. That would be an abuse of a position of trust.

THE DANGEROUS INVOLVEMENT

We now come to the real danger zone! A chapter of this title *must* consider the problem of becoming too involved with the married partner of the opposite sex—the single woman with the husband, the single man with the wife. This kind of attachment is more insidious, and possibly more common, than those we have already considered, so it needs frank treatment.

Where a marriage is really secure, the danger of wrongful attachments is not a great threat. It is probably minimal but, distant though the threat may be, it is always there. Perhaps it is right to recognise, at the outset of this discussion that *no one* is immune from this danger. The *real* danger, however, is when a marriage is already insecure with emotional rocks in evidence that a single friend of either sex may be a real hazard. Married friends can of course be just as much of a danger, but we are considering singleness here and must therefore concern ourselves with the problem of the married man who has fallen in love with a single girl, or the wife who has fallen for a bachelor friend.

Rarely is such a situation calculated or premeditated. Rarely does a single person set out to lure the wife or attract the husband away from the partner, or *vice versa*. There are presumably a few who set out, in cold blood, to wreck a marriage, but, more often, such situations develop slowly with enough good in the relationship to blind the friends to its dangers. The husband may, at first, regard the single woman friend as a sister or the wife look on the single man as a brother. Then as affection deepens, there may come a point where it is as though someone has 'switched the rails' and the whole relationship changes course.

This sort of involvement is very common — more common than is sometimes realised. For those who have had a particular moral upbringing, to get snarled up in such a relationship can produce enormous guilt feelings. They arise because the relationship seems to be transgressing moral standards, so there are guilt feelings towards the rightful partner; guilt feelings because of the need for secrecy; and guilt feelings arising from the erroneous idea that it is a unique situation.

In some ways it is understandable when this kind of problem

arises. It may be a small consolation to the wife to realise that the qualities that so attracted her to her husband in the first place are still there and are attractive to other women. In addition, married life will probably have mellowed him and given him extra charm so making him even more lovable. She can rightly take some pride for her share in that! The husband might be flattered to think that other men find his wife attractive and warmhearted, that they admire (even envy him) for having made such a conquest; that marriage far from causing his wife to lose those things which first drew him has, in fact, enhanced them, and that there is an added bloom upon her now that she is a wife and mother.

Such thoughts will not give real comfort if the whole situation gets out of hand and the relationship develops in such a way that either the husband or wife feels excluded, or the marriage is in real danger. What is the right course to take in that kind of situation? No one answer can meet all the possibilities. The obvious thing might be to end the relationship as soon as one becomes aware of what is happening, in fact to carry out the sort of surgery described in Matthew 5:29: 'If your eye offends you, pluck it out and cast it from you . . . if your hand offends you, cut it off . . . ' It would be such a complete solution, so sensible, so effective, but it is usually far from easy. The entanglements are often more like a growth that has spread throughout the body than like a limb that can be neatly hacked off.

How can one ease oneself out of a relationship before things have gone too far without hurting the family as a whole? How are the children's questions to be answered? What reasons can one give for breaking the friendship? If the real reasons are given, is confidence between the husband and wife going to be shattered for good? Can one present the facts to the other partner one has also come to love, without the human frailty in the situation appearing as outsized treachery on the part of their friend and spouse? Would the 'innocent party' ever be able to believe that it was not deliberate disloyalty? Would the injured husband or wife be able to recognise any ways in which first, he or she may have contributed to the problem, and secondly, ways in which they might be able to remedy it?

However the truth comes out—whether it is accidentally discovered or whether it is presented by the 'guilty' pair in an attempt to be honest and repair the friendship before it becomes irreparable—it is bound to bring pain. One might shrink from bringing such a problem into the open for the very reason that it would give such hurt to the rightful partner. He or she may feel that the friend has acted treacherously—perhaps he has—and place all the blame on the friend rather than on the partner, for this is easier to bear. It is possible to break a friendship but far more devastating to end a marriage. In all the searing pain and humiliation of the moment of truth, the 'injured party' may lose perspective. It has to be remembered that it is not treacherous to love, only to rob and destroy. If one is seeking a positive solution rather than one that will have lastingly unhappy memories, somehow the love must be allowed to continue and grow in a *rightful* way and all involved will need help to see that the proper channel is found.

It is sadly true that few single people would be altruistic enough to think *only* of the good of the family or the 'innocent' husband or wife (inverted commas are used because, in this discussion, I am assuming a loving relationship between a married person and a single person, but not an adulterous one). Suddenly alight with the joy that newly awakened love brings, in one sense it is the very last thing that they want to stop. Yet they may hate the deception, hate the guilt feelings, hate the knowledge that they are wronging someone they love. Often they really do want to do the right thing by everyone, including themselves, but selfishness is so very deep in all of us and makes it so easy to rationalise the situation. If one could have a bugging device that picked up the inner conversation, we should probably hear something like this:

'Of course it would be wrong just to abandon my friends. After all, love is God-given and therefore in itself cannot be wrong. Keep it pure and it can be a wonderful thing for all concerned. It will make me an altogether more loving person in every area of my life. I shall be a more complete person knowing that I love and am loved—and that surely will have its overspill of joy and usefulness to others. I can contribute to the marriage by giving something to the husband that his wife is not able to give him (or to the wife that her husband is not giving her) and this will make it easier for them to stay together in a deeper companionship. I may be bringing a fullness to their life that might otherwise be missing. As long as we don't commit adultery or transgress our moral standards, surely it isn't wrong to love each other?'

So the reasoning might continue its devious route. Obviously it would be better not to become involved in the first place in the kind of relationship that raises questions and threatens to hurt friends, and, as I have said, it does not usually happen intentionally. How then can one avoid this pitfall without keeping one's husband-friends, or wife-friends at arm's length? There are some 'do's and don'ts' to bear in mind. Here are five 'don'ts' to be observed when with a married person of the opposite sex.

Don't discuss intimacies;
Don't listen to complaints;
Don't arbitrate in quarrels;
Don't be too much of a willing sympathiser;
Don't offer advice (concerning the marriage and its
   relationship).

To be too ready with sympathy may lead to a desire to offer physical comfort. That can break down further barriers of reserve and there may follow criticisms of and comparisons with the other partner. If tender, kindly treatment uncovers a real need in the friend and you discover you are meeting it, it takes almost brutality to stop, refusing any more such ministrations either then or on future occasions. If the restraints I have mentioned are not being heeded in a friendship, then it has entered 'the danger zone'. No effort should be spared to restore perspective and divert love back into its rightful channel or someone is going to be badly hurt, probably all three people involved.

I have spoken of the pain and rejection a single person may feel at being 'thrown out' of a relationship. How can we describe the pain between a husband and wife when their marriage seems in jeopardy, when they lose respect for each other, when one feels desperate and the other feels trapped? The woman will think of the children and her maternal instincts of preservation will come to the fore. She may fight like a wild cat to save the marriage — and that can be degrading, pathetic and altogether distasteful.

'THE THREEFOLD CORD'

There have been cases where a single person has loved one of a marriage partnership with the full cognizance and blessing of the other partner — but such cases are very exceptional. So unusual is it that a whole book was devoted to one such relationship.[1] It tells how three people, who lived together in a bond of deep love, walked the tight rope of a threefold relationship, for, not only did Hudson Shaw and Maude Royden love each other deeply, they were 'in love' and Effie Shaw knew it and encouraged it.

'If Hudson and I knew our minds, she (Effie) knew our hearts . . . she believed that I could never have all I needed as long as Hudson gave to me, and I to him, no more than affection, no more than friendship.'[2]

Many a woman might recognise that her single friend 'could never have all she needed' without the love of a man, but she would not necessarily be prepared for her husband to be that man — and one could scarcely blame her.

There are few women or men who can face the thought of

[1] Dr. Maude Royden, *The Threefold Cord* (Gollancz).
[2] Ibid., p. 25.

another giving to the one they love even what they themselves cannot give and do not want. This is where Effie Shaw
was apart from the rest of us. She did not wish her husband
and her friend to transgress their moral standards or hers:
she did want us to have all that was possible for us—not only
love but passionate love.

I marvel as I write. Will anyone believe that she was never
jealous of our love? Perhaps not: yet it is true. She never
was. I am certain she never had to fight against jealousy and
never felt it . . . She understood our deepest need and met it
without effort, with the perfection that can only come from
perfect love.[1]

This example is cited not to calm uneasy consciences, nor to
provide a loophole for those in wrongful relationships, but to
show that there are exceptional cases where people find themselves in a triangular relationship that is not necessarily sinful
or altogether sinful. There are Christian people who are prepared to take this risk and apparently can do so with a clear
conscience before God, but it is an enormous risk. It seems that
a few can find love of this sort a real blessing and fulfilment,
but have a care in this respect. The Effies of this world are very,
very rare.

Maude Royden herself makes it plain that her relationship
with the Shaws was only possible because there was no guilty
secret to be kept. Without real openness, it could only have led
to disaster.

From the beginning there were three of us. That made
possible everything that was impossible. Hudson and I knew
that we must always think of life as including all three. We
must never think of any other relationship but this. This
was to be our life: Hudson, Effie and I. It was not so hard
after all. It would indeed have been not hard but simply
impossible (being what we are) to have a furtive love affair.

[1] Ibid., p. 27.

How hateful it sounds! Perhaps it should not: There are men and women who do not find it so . . . I say only that secrecy to us was impossible . . .

She scolded us when we fell short of the love she imagined for us. She wept when we were angry or ungracious to each other. She made Hudson promise that, if she died, he would marry me 'at once' — without waiting — 'not troubling about what people said of us'. How little we thought how and when we should fulfil her wish! For whatever she said we knew that we must never think such thoughts. We must be always three. That was our safety.[1]

There are few married women who could be so free from jealousy and there are few single people who could love in this way either; few who could be so selfless that, in these circumstances, they would not inwardly long for times when it could be a twosome rather than a threesome; few who could be completely honest with themselves and with each other; few who would not wonder, as Hudson Shaw himself did, 'if it was right to give to anyone any part of what, in a perfect marriage, belongs to the wife, even if the marriage was not perfect and what was given to another was only a part'.[2]

However beautiful the friendship, however open and honest, indeed however enriching, there is still a sense in which it is poaching on another's territory. For most people, rather than seeking to be one of the few exceptions to the rule, it is better to recognise that we are on forbidden ground and direct the love back into its proper channel where that rightful loving, already spoken of, can find its free and full outlet. We may try to justify the poaching principle. We may find every reason why it is legitimate, but ultimately for the Christian, there is only one answer. It *is* poaching on someone else's territory.

A practical step that may be a help to a single woman who finds her love for a married man growing apace would be to

[1] *The Threefold Cord*, pp. 28–29.
[2] Ibid., p. 31.

cultivate a friendship with his wife; not to get a firmer leverage in their home and thus have further opportunities of seeing him, but rather to get to know her *for her own sake*. There is, in a threefold relationship, a need to cultivate a friendship with the husband and wife separately, *and* together.

A friend once told me that she grew to love deeply a man whom she often met in a working capacity. Both were involved in the same kind of church work so they met at meetings and sat on the same committees. They had a tremendous respect for one another and a real affinity with each other. Sometimes they travelled together and had working lunches together, and the friendship was a mutually good thing. Then came the invitations home to meet his wife—for meals, to stay after committees, or on a free weekend. It was a thoroughly happy relationship which all three enjoyed and which proved a growing point for them all. The wife, in this case, was well aware of the mutual admiration and respect between the single friend and her husband, but she was secure in herself and did not feel excluded. She could well see how her husband appreciated the kinship of mind and heart he had with this particular woman.

My friend told me how, if she were to stay with them for a weekend, she would try, quite deliberately, to take an earlier train from town than the husband—though they could quite easily have travelled together—in order to have some time alone with the wife. 'After a cuppa and a good natter, we would go up to the bedroom and look through the wardrobe at her new clothes or the bargains she had bought for the house. We would experiment with make-up and have a wonderful time enjoying those feminine things that you can't do when there's a man around.' When he eventually came home, it would be to find two women very happy in *their* friendship, and himself being drawn into it. Thus she had a friendship with them separately and together, and that is an important one to remember.

If a single woman only visits a home when the husband is

there, then she must not be surprised if the wife grows a little uneasy and perhaps suspicious. It is a good thing to plan a visit sometimes knowing full well that the husband will be away— not to keep suspicions at bay but because there is real enjoyment in getting to know the wife in her own right, and coming to love her for herself. It is right to share some confidences with the wife (even if later she decides to share them with her husband). It is right to honour her for her own importance and worth and to let her feel that she can be trusted. It is decidedly disturbing for her if the single friend only confides in her husband and that when they are alone. Here too there is a need for sharing separately and together. Sometimes it is the most natural thing to share a confidence with them as a couple. Other times the nature of the confidence requires a one-to-one sharing, for an audience of two would be rather overwhelming. The nature of the confidence will normally decide when the sharing should be with one partner or the other.

What of those relationships where commonsense, caution, wisdom and discipline have been found wanting? It is all very well to talk of seeing the danger and avoiding it. What if one has been foolish enough not to realise the danger and has met it head on, now only to find oneself up to the neck in that bitter-sweet emotional admixture of a triangular relationship? It can be a long, hard road back to rightful relationships with some deaths and resurrections in the realms of desire and will. For the Christian, however, there are some clear guides.

To be in love with someone else's husband or wife in a secretive way, to be arranging clandestine meetings, to be sharing a deep level of intimacy (even if that does not include physical intimacy) cannot really be 'walking in the light'. This means that every part of life must be open and transparent. There must be 'truth in the inward parts', if one really wants to mature as a Christian. To have areas where the light of God is consciously withheld will inevitably prevent growth.

A number of friends have told me that it was on this very point that they foundered. Ultimately they could not bear 'all that deception'—deception where the wife was concerned, where other friends and business associates were involved *and*, stupidly, an attempted deception in the face of God. More than that, we need to remember that the people we most easily deceive are, of course, ourselves.

The advocates of 'situation ethics' have encouraged a lot of fluffy thinking in this respect. It is absolutely true that love is the all-important thing in all our actions. That is borne out by the teaching of our Lord himself. It is true we need to face our responsibilities in deciding for ourselves what is the most loving thing to do in any given situation rather than looking for an ABC of human relationships or a Highway Code for Conduct that spells out the right and wrong of every action. That would only lead to infantilism or to the kind of legalism that Jesus so abhorred in the Pharisees, the harsh, calculating rectitude that knows nothing of the mercy of God. The 'situationists' are right to remind us of our personal responsibility in deciding on the most loving course and, just because we are all so very different, we shall not always agree what that course is. We are not allowed unlimited private judgment however, for the Holy Spirit is our teacher who educates our consciences. Those friends who confessed that they 'could not stand all that deception any longer' were, in fact, acknowledging the work of the Holy Spirit in their lives. He eventually moves in on a wrong relationship and quickens the conscience till it becomes exceedingly tender. Every 'word from the Lord' in the Scriptures, in sermons, in prayers then seems to accuse us. Peace of mind and heart only comes with the final yielding to His sovereignty. Since the Holy Spirit is so gracious, so truly courteous and since he so respects individual freedom, he never bulldozes us into submission. The pressure may at first be very gentle. It is the patient insistence in the heart that truly longs to be in the path of God's choosing, that tells in the long run. For what he does is to offer us not the equivalent of a summons, a court proceeding and a fine, but *a learning oppor-tunity* that is itself a loving, growing thing. We must, however, be willing to co-operate with Him.

Conversely there is the danger of becoming over-scrupulous in the matter of relationships. We may be so aware of the dangers that we are afraid to be outgoing enough towards people of the opposite sex. It would be sad indeed if, by what has gone before in this chapter, single people began to feel worried about all their relationships with married couples. To allow a free flow of love may involve some risks but they can be supported if the necessary cautions are observed too. Some-times a relationship comes near to the danger zone but is righted before it is too late. There is no need then to feel guilty. Remember that the Holy Spirit focuses his burning ray on the deception, not the loving. No experience of *true* loving is wasted. Often one can look back on a relationship that, if it had developed, promised to be illicit. Yet there were moments in that relationship that brought new insights and new love that will undoubtedly be enriching in the future both to oneself and to one's understanding of others.

No experience of *true* loving . . . perhaps it is right just to spell out what is meant here by 'true loving'. Clearly it is no wishy-washy, sentimental or self-seeking thing. Even if our loving is free of lust, it may still be selfish. The love that God gives is the love that He Himself has for us — holy love, free from all self-seeking or impurity.

A love that is warm, tender and outgoing, that wants the highest and best for others, that is not afraid to express itself in all the legitimate ways open to it, a love which can stand the searchlight beam of God's holiness and not shrivel — that is the love that we must aim at and seek to make our ethic in every situation. That sort of love scarcely leaves room for any furtive relationship.

There have been countless people who have made mistakes in loving but who have got back 'on course'. Here is the testimony of one woman who became enmeshed in a relationship with a married man and who was trying to work through it with a responsible Christian attitude. She writes:

I prayed constantly—
   that the love should be hallowed;
   that it would make me more loving towards others;
   that we should be preserved from adultery;
   that his wife and children should not be hurt;
   that there should never be any scandal;
   that we should not abuse the gift of love which we felt
   sure was given by God.

God in His mercy, answered all of those prayers in some measure. It was certainly right and important to open up areas of the relationship to God, but it still meant that some basic issues went unsolved and therefore left a certain unreality in the prayer. The one prayer that should have been prayed was left unspoken. I never once prayed, 'Lord, show me how to end this relationship'. On the contrary, I asked to be shown how it could continue without falling into sin. There's a masterful piece of self deception! We *were* already sinning. I sometimes dared to say to Almighty God 'You can have the key to every other room in my life—but not this one!'

Ultimately of course He put His finger on that very room and said 'That one. That's the one I want above all others.' It had never occurred to me before that sometimes, more than anything else, He wants us to give Him our sin. But I wanted to keep a hold on the sin I loathed yet loved.

At last under the loving pressure of the Holy Spirit I yielded. Though at first there was a terrible emptiness, gradually there came a transference of dependence and love to God Himself and I marvelled at His patience that for so many years had been prepared to be robbed, that had bided the time till the Holy Spirit had finished His inner and hidden work and could at last bring me to a point of fuller surrender. I stood in wonder and love before the God who would not wrest the relationship from me and nip it in the bud, but who waited patiently till the time came when I could learn most from the termination.

MAKING THE BREAK

How then does one make the actual break? How does one face the future again?

One conductor of a retreat gave a rather harsh and unhelpful piece of advice (the conductor was a woman, and the retreatants mainly single women missionary candidates). 'If you have the will to fall in love,' she said, 'you must exercise the same will to fall out of love.' This was nearly as helpful as saying, 'If you open Pandora's box, then you must find a way of closing it.'

More helpful it would seem is the story that Corrie Ten Boom tells in *The Hiding Place*[1] of her own disappointment in love and the way she offered up her broken heart. The circumstances were quite different in that she had fallen in love with a man while he was still single (and had understood the love to be mutual). Then without warning he arrived on the doorstep arm in arm with his new wife. The shock and bewilderment made Corrie reel. She fled to her room to come to terms with the pain, anguish and grief. How was she to cope with the situation? What was she to do with her love for him? These were questions she asked herself. Should she let her love turn to anger, resentment and sourness? It would have been a tragedy if she had. Eventually she came to the place where she could pray for them both with real love and ask for the blessing of God on *their* marriage.

A moving story has been condensed into a few sentences but perhaps even this summary will convey something of the triumph of it. For surely nothing but the grace of God can

[1] Corrie Ten Boom, *The Hiding Place* (Hodder and Stoughton).

enable one woman to pray for the happiness and enrichment of another woman who stands in the place where she would love to be? Yet this is precisely what Corrie did.

To some this may sound like a comfortless counsel of perfection. 'It may be possible for Corrie Ten Boom,' they will explode, 'but not for me!' And one can sympathise with that point of view. It is so easy to feel cheated and to hear oneself bursting out with 'How unfair of God!' The need to terminate a relationship can bring a great complexity of emotion towards Him. Why, if He gives love, does He then ask for it back? Why does He cause to cross my path a man I could love utterly and completely, but who is already married? It is a comfort to remember that the greatness of God's love is such that if we need to vent our feelings of anger and let-down on Him, we can do so. It is right that we do this rather than push them down in to ourselves or transform them into emotions of bitterness. We shall not be punished for exposing negative feelings towards God. We do not have to come to Him on our best behaviour or in our party dress. He wants to meet with us as we are. If this means coming sometimes with anger and fury, He is big enough to contain this. His constant loving of us is of such a quality that it will not stop because of our invectives. It is better for us to get our wretched feelings out rather than repress them. God even wants our apparently unacceptable feelings. He wants the lot!

Could it be that people are loth to terminate a triangular relationship because they fear they will not find enough love from other sources to meet their need? If so, to what extent is this fear justified? Is it true? Unfortunately we cannot say, '*of course* love will come from other sources'. There is no 'of course' about it. Love will only be received in proportion to the love that is given. After the termination of a friendship, almost the last thing one can do is be outgoing in love. One is too sore, numb and sometimes angry. It might be possible to resort to a married couple or a friend, share with them what has happened, and *trust* them to accept one as one is without frills and

polished manners. Perhaps it would be a helpful word to
married couples to remind them of the importance of the grace
of acceptance. If, for example, a single woman comes to you
brokenhearted and in trouble, it is not the time for homilies
and good advice. If she is in a state of shock (as is possible),
then it is highly unlikely that she will be in a fit mood to listen
to advice anyway. Her need is simply to know that someone
cares for her and loves her as she is, without judgment or
condemnation.

Eventually the time may come when the single friend will be
glad to sit down and talk and think the problem through with
you. If the turn-about, the clean break, hasn't actually taken
place, she may need you to stand by her in loving support as
she braces herself for the dreaded moment.

There can be a real sense of grief and mourning when a
relationship is ended. It is partly the price, and partly the
inevitable consequence of a love that cannot find fulfilment.
If a single person is talking it through with a friend, it is less
than helpful if the friend pulls in premature comfort with, for
example, 'It'll all be fine!' because it just won't. It takes
months, even years, to get over such separations. The longer the
relationship has gone on, the longer will the period of grieving
last.

There are those, however, who have suffered this kind of
radical surgery who find that, some time after the event, they
can really say that there was a form of relief and release in the
termination. Look at it honestly and realistically. To continue
an illicit relationship (knowing what the outcome will be) is
very much a hand to mouth existence, 'topping up' our needs
as and when we can. Having known love, we know how lovely
it can be and feel we cannot do without it. We dare not risk
losing this particular source, lest we find no others. Yet because
we are only topping up and living in a state of unreality, we are
afraid to sit down and think about it too much. This can lead to
emotional weariness, a sense of secrecy, unhappiness in prayer

life, and finding oneself captive to the priorities of each day rather than letting the priorities speak for themselves.

This is not liberty—the liberty that true love should bring. In fact, it is a form of bondage and brings great restrictions, worry and frustration.

Any who stand halfway between two opinions about a triangular relationship, any who fear to make a break lest they should be left destitute of love altogether, would perhaps be helped by pondering the words of C. Day Lewis:

> Selfhood begins with the walking away
> And love is proved in the letting go.[1]

A QUESTIONNAIRE FOR SINGLE WOMEN WHO FIND THEMSELVES IN A TRIANGULAR FRIENDSHIP.

1. *Is my love inclusive?*

Do I know the wives of my men friends? How well do I know them? and how well do they know me?

Do I make a deliberate attempt to cultivate friendship with them?

Do I really enjoy being with them for their own sakes or is it just a necessary formality in order to preserve my friendship with their husbands?

How far am I able really to share with the wife in a triangular friendship?

Are there areas of my relationship with her husband which I would have reservations about sharing?

2. *Is my love truly sensitive?*

If the wife is ill, do I rush round to look after the family, do some cooking, clean the house, cope with the washing and ironing? Good and well intentioned as these may be, have I really stopped to consider how the wife feels about it? Is she really relieved to have someone step in and manage, or does it

[1] C. Day Lewis, 'The Walking Away'.

make her feel hopelessly inadequate? Would it be kinder to leave the house in a muddle for a while, or would *that* secretly worry her? Do I know *her* needs, or am I confusing them with my own—my need to be a tower of strength? Is a bouncing, healthy, capable single woman just about the last straw for her?

If the wife has to go away, am I very quick to offer to entertain her husband and children? What are my motives for doing so? Is it really to help the wife, or to demonstrate how competent I am to cook a marvellous meal, act as a hostess, cope with the children, and do so looking neat and attractive, at the same time keeping up an interesting conversation? Do I hope that, by the end of the evening the husband will be filled with admiration thinking, 'What a wonderful wife she will make someone, some day?'

Am I sensitive about accounting to the wife for any extra time I *have* to spend with her husband—either in working or travelling?

3. *Is my love selfless and unpossessive?*

Is there any area in which I feel jealous of the wife—of her home, security, status, material possessions?

Am I envious of her right to sexual love?

Do I allow my imagination to think of them when they are alone? Does it stray into the privacy of their bedroom? Do I make mental substitutions and thereby commit adultery of the heart and mind?

Do I embarrass them by showering gifts upon them more to satisfy my own longing to give than their need to receive?

Am I happy to baby-sit for them and really rejoice that they can have an evening out together?

When my own needs are clamouring insistently, do I really love them enough to put their needs before mine?

A questionnaire such as this is not meant to provide a list of 'do's and don'ts'. It should not be used as a rigorous examination paper to test the chastity of our thoughts. Rather it is a check list to help us understand our motives more clearly and to show those areas that may need to be watched and understood further—the areas that *could* be dangerous. Even in formulating such a list, one knows that there is the risk that some may use it rather like those little books aimed to help people prepare for confession. Some fall into the trap of working through the list and admitting to every sin. It is rather like the little boy who confessed every sin in the book including the fact that he had been 'published and printed by the Church Union'.[1]

---

[1] Colin Stephenson, *Merrily on High* (D.C.T.), p. 43.

CHAPTER SIX

To Each his Gift

ONE OF THE PARTICULAR CATEGORIES OF THOSE WHO WALK alone is of those who have deliberately chosen to be single. A good deal of prominence has been given to the subject of celibacy recently, mainly because of happenings within the Roman Catholic church. Much publicity has been given to those priests who have renounced their vows of chastity. Because of this, there may be a feeling among some lay people that celibacy is a harsh imposition laid on all Roman Catholic priests and accepted by them grudgingly and in great sorrow. No one renounces marriage for whatever reason, without *some* heartache. But there are few single people who renounce their particular freedom for marriage without pangs of real pain! Because there are those pangs it does not necessarily mean that the celibate life is one of lifelong bitterness, or that marriage is an irksome bondage. Both states bring their own renunciations as well as their joys.

In criticising celibacy, people sometimes say: 'But it is so unnatural!' Of course it is. So is much else in the Christian life. In our fallen humanity it is not natural to love those who are your enemies, pray for those who persecute you, turn the other cheek and accept further humiliation, lop off wrongful relationships with one fell swoop as with a surgeon's knife. Yet this is the standard set by Christ and those in his family are called to rise to it. This is the important part, however. *Every time a call is given, a gift is offered with it.* The call to the 'unnatural' life that is set out in the Sermon on the Mount could not be fully accepted unless there was also given the gift of the Christ-life in us. For all who are truly called to the life of celibacy, there is also the accompanying grace-gift.

In I Corinthians 7, Paul makes it quite clear that celibacy is a gift of grace and not a matter of effort or merit. When he then counsels each one to have his own wife or husband in order to avoid the danger of misconduct, he is not, as some seem to think, making concessions for those who are less holy and unable to contain their passions. He is simply acknowledging that the grace-gift of celibacy is not given to all, any more than the gifts of administration or teaching are given to all. He argues that it is ridiculous—even wrong—for anyone deliberately to refrain from marriage and its proper expressions of love *unless* they have the gift. Celibacy, therefore, should not be thought of merely as a giving up, but rather as a taking on, a receiving of a gift. Viewed rightly it can be seen as something gloriously positive, something related to the Kingdom of God, to Christ, and to the mission of the Church, and a means of great liberation.

Not surprisingly, the reasons for celibacy and its purpose are puzzling to many laymen. It often seems to them an unnecessary waste. Let us look at it more deeply, then.

To be properly understood, celibacy needs to be seen within the context of the biblical teaching on marriage. Marriage under the old covenant was vitally important for the People of God and for their furtherance as a religious body. It was obligatory for Jews to marry, a very solemn obligation from which only travelling rabbis were exempt. So, although celibacy was a very rare thing in the Jewish religion, our Lord was able to remain single without breaking the Law. It was not that he deprecated marriage—as is clear from his teaching in Mark 10:6 when he answers the question of the Pharisees on divorce:

8

'What did Moses say about divorce?' Jesus asked them.

'He said it was all right,' they replied. 'He said that all a man has to do is write his wife a letter of dismissal.'

'And why did he say that?' Jesus asked. 'I'll tell you why—it was a concession to your hard-hearted wickedness. But it certainly isn't God's way. For from the very first He made men and women to be joined together permanently in marriage; therefore a man is to leave his mother and father, and he and his wife are united so that they are no longer two, but one. And no man separates what God has joined together.'

Our Lord also used marriage as an analogy of his relation to his people. He is the bridegroom who encourages feasting and joy. St. Paul takes up the same symbolism in his letter to the Ephesians (Eph. 5:22–32) where he speaks of the mystery of the union between Christ and his church in terms of marriage.

There is, however, a new element in the teaching of the New Testament on this subject. Under the old covenant, marriage was vitally related to the continuing life of Israel. But with the coming of Christ, there is a new situation for the signs of the Last Days and the Kingdom of God are at work.

Marriage is exalted but differently expressed. Membership of the People of God is no longer by means of natural procreation within Israel, but by supernatural rebirth in the Church. The Christian no longer lives merely within the order of creation, but also within the order of redemption. The emphasis now is not only on natural procreation for the continuity and multiplication of the People of God, but also on renunciation for the sake of the Kingdom of Heaven.[1]

The question that is relevant to our discussion is this: How far should renunciation be accepted today for the sake of the Kingdom of Heaven, and does this affect our thinking about

[1] D. W. Allen, Unpublished Lectures.

celibacy? Does Christ still ask men and women to accept this calling to a way of life specially adapted to the service of the Kingdom? If so, in what ways does celibacy further its work?

It is necessary to define what is meant here by celibacy. The Oxford Dictionary says that it is 'abstinence (especially as an obligation or principle) from marriage; unmarried life'. Such a definition could cover both those who deliberately abstain from marriage by a vow of chastity, *and* those who, as the years unfold, gradually discover that the will of God for them is singleness and accept it as His gift to them (though, to be honest, few of us in this second category have been able to accept it as a gift with immediate alacrity. It has been a growing acceptance and appreciation!)

For the purposes of this chapter however, we shall use the term 'celibacy' to signify those who, in obedience to what they believe is a call of God to them, have vowed to remain single. Sometimes this is a vow which is made publicly to God in the presence of representatives of His Church, as at a profession ceremony in a Religious Community where it is made along with the vows of poverty and obedience. Some priests take this vow at their ordination while others make it in a private service. Some never make any explicit vow but acknowledge from the beginning that theirs is to be a life of openness and that availability of a special sort which, in all probability, will involve singleness. There are, too, laymen and women who enter into a commitment with the full understanding that this will mean the single life. Therefore we are considering in this chapter those who are single by decision rather than by discovery.

We accept that, in some secular callings, especially those of a highly dangerous character, it is expedient for a man to be single. In some jobs a married man would expose his wife and family either to great risk or to great anxiety. Sometimes explorers, test-pilots, scientists, etc., have accepted a voluntary celibacy for the furtherance of the work of science, industry, geography or technology. It is this same unattachedness that some feel called to offer to God. The practical advantages are many.

In discussing the indissolubility of marriage, the disciples so reacted to the difficulties in such a way of life, that Jesus was led to say: 'There be eunuchs, which have made themselves eunuchs for the Kingdom of Heaven's sake. He that is able to receive it, let him receive it.' Some have interpreted this passage as having meaning only for the very earliest Christians, who believed in Christ's imminent return, but no meaning for the present day. Perhaps we need to think very carefully before we rule out altogether the value of celibacy in terms of the Kingdom today.

The celibate priest is obviously free in a way that the married priest is not free. He is more available, and is also freer to accept hospitality from his people and share in their home life in a way that is a comfort to him and a joy to them. It is easier to house a single man than a married man and a family! Sometimes clergy are able to share a clergy house, or a single priest may be able to live in a fairly modest flat. In these days of housing difficulties, this is a not unimportant consideration. The financial burden upon the church is lessened, perhaps releasing money for needy causes. This is not to suggest that the celibate should be kept on a miserable pittance. A labourer is worthy of his hire. But he may be a labourer who feels he is able to accept a far smaller stipend than some, because his family commitments are not heavy. The labourer with a wife and five children needs a fairly substantial income. If it is not substantial enough, he can be subjected to serious financial worries.

The responsibilities of the married man must also include sensible provision for the future. For many clergy this is one of the biggest problems. When the house goes with the job, there is always the thought: 'If anything happens to me, what of my wife and children? Where will they live? How can I provide security for them when it is hard to make ends meet now?' Most people in their middle years have begun, if not finished, buying a house. For many in the Christian ministry the question of how to buy a home for retirement is one that is filled with dread.

The celibate man is also more mobile. It is far easier to send him on some special mission or uproot him for a particular job than to move an entire family, with all that that involves in the way of moving house and changing schools.

SPIRITUAL ADVANTAGES AND DISADVANTAGES

Besides the practical advantages of celibacy within the Christian ministry, there are many spiritual advantages too. It does not automatically follow that the unmarried priest cares more for the things of the Lord, as St. Paul argues in I Corinthians 7, but he has the chance to do so. Generally speaking, he should have more time and emotional energy for pastoral work. This is not to imply that married priests neglect their pastoral duties — some are so zealous that it is their family duties that they neglect. But there must inevitably be times of great tension when it is extremely difficult to see one's priorities. The married priest may sometimes feel trapped into an unavoidable neglect of his wife and family. Some do succeed magnificently in their family life and are far better pastors as a result. The richness of their own married life increases their capacity to love and overflows to their people, bringing mutual joy.

Sometimes when an unmarried priest seems diffident and unapproachable, people comment that what he needs is a wife. Marriage would help him to blossom out, they say. This would not necessarily be so. There are many shy and diffident married clergy. One thing *is* certain, and it is this. If celibacy is a true gift, then it should not make a man dry and unloving. It should make him more warm-hearted and outgoing than he would otherwise have been. His love which goes out to so many with a prodigality not possible to those who have an exclusive relationship, means that he is often greatly loved in return. The giving and receiving of much love can do nothing else but enlarge his heart.

We have spoken of practical and spiritual advantages of celibacy, though not of the disadvantages. There are undoubtedly some. It must not be thought however that the acceptance of celibacy is a way of seeking greater tranquillity and freedom from marital cares and responsibilities. The true gift of celibacy is not governed by selfish motives but by a desire to follow a particular call for the sake of the Kingdom of God. In marriage there is a renunciation of unattachedness while, in celibacy there is a renunciation of a particular kind of human companionship and marital joy. Both are ways of serving the Lord. Neither is superior to the other. The celibate is simply freeing himself in a particular way to give all his strength and care to the proclamation of the Gospel.

Celibacy, which deprives a man of marital intimacy and of fatherhood — important sacrifices — enables him in return to devote himself more completely to people's cares, to their salvation and sanctification. Since he has no exclusive love, the Christian celibate can always be at everyone's disposal, and he has the time and interior freedom to serve his neighbour — whoever he may be — in charity. He has the opportunity of giving plenty of time to anyone who wishes to confide in him and he can devote much attention to the care of people who need his prolonged help. Besides, his solitude often gives confidence to those who wish to make their confession to him. It is nonsense to think that he cannot understand men because he does not live like many of them, in difficult marital or family circumstances. It is not necessary to have experienced all human situations in order to be guided by the Holy Spirit in the direction of souls. Specially fitted to a ministry of spiritual direction, in whatever form it may be, the Christian celibate will find the fulfilment of the hundredfold promise made by Christ (Mark 10:29-30 and parallels). He experiences a spiritual fatherhood of those who freely confide in him in his solitude.[1]

In I Corinthians 7:26, St. Paul writes: 'I suppose therefore that this is good for the present distress, I say, that it is good for a man so to be (in celibacy).' Here Paul is not stressing celibacy for its own intrinsic value but as a positive stand in the face of contemporary problems ... unfaithfulness in marriage, permissiveness in society, a form of situation ethic that turned law not into grace but into licence, abuse of the body and misuse of other material gifts. It all sounds horribly familiar. In the light of *our* contemporary problems, so akin in many ways to those of the Corinthians, would Paul find a meaningful role for the celibate today?

LAY CELIBATES

It is not only within the ordained ministry that people are feeling that they want to share in the work of the Kingdom in this particular way. Sometimes laymen voluntarily accept celibacy for life, and they must not be confused with those who over the years come to an acceptance of their singleness as part of the will and purpose of God for their lives.

In *The New Nuns* Michael Novak writes of the decision of five attractive Roman Catholic girls who went to Oklahoma City to lead a celibate, dedicated Christian life together and to work individually for various Christian ends. The five are not nuns and hate to be thought of as nuns. To them the word has overtones of institutions and rules. They want to lead a celibate life nourished by a common life in a Christian household. One girl said, 'I want my life to speak to people of more than just me—of Christ. Not in words, but by something in myself. I want to speak as a healthy woman, as someone happy, fulfilled. I've chosen to be single. For me the Association is a way of life,

[1] Max Thurian, *Marriage and Celibacy* (S.C.M.), p. 108.

the way I choose to love and to grow in love, to love Christ.'[1]

Another example where lay-religious have voluntarily accepted celibacy, to be available to all, is seen in such communities as The Little Brothers of Jesus and the Little Sisters of Jesus. These small communities are seeking to live out their religious vocations in industrial areas in as close an identification to their neighbours as is possible. Wearing ordinary working clothes, they carry out a normal day's work but return to the Community house—in some cases an ordinary terraced house—to share their meals, their worship, their life.

The Grail is a further example. Here is a group of Roman Catholic lay women who are in the forefront of the re-education of Catholics and who are doing so much ecumenically that it is amazing what they can fit into their twenty-four hours.

These are only a few of countless attempts to follow our Lord in this particular path for the sake of the Kingdom. They may say something important about the way in which celibates should live. There certainly are times when 'it is not good that man should be alone'. Perhaps celibate clergy should consider carefully the possibilities of living in some kind of informal community so that, as the American girl said, the 'celibate life can be nourished by the common life in a Christian household'.

THE CALL TO CELIBACY

If celibacy is a vocation, how does the call of God become clear? Max Thurian has said in *Marriage and Celibacy*.[2]

The call and gift of God are in the first place revealed by the interior witness of the Holy Spirit; this produces joy and peace in the consideration and the choice of one vocation rather than another. In this there is no rational criterion, only a simple assurance of faith. It should be added that celibacy is only a circumstance, a state, and a position

[1] Michael Novak, *The New Nuns*, Sheed and Ward.
[2] *Marriage and Celibacy*, p. 86.

demanded by a call of God which is greater and more complex — a special mission or a difficult ministry which would make family life impossible and which requires complete unattachedness; a life of contemplation or study which calls for entire freedom of spirit; life in a regular community for the sake or witness of a freely available ministry in the Church. So celibacy cannot be considered as a vocation for its own sake, but only in terms of a special service for God. Again it should be considered not as a demand or as an obligation, but as a way of life for which graces are created so that a man may accept it and persevere in it.

As in other vocations, the circumstances of life can be a guide. St. Paul sees the providence of God (I Corinthians 7:17-24) hacking a path through the jungle of choices open to a man. But even when a man has considered these carefully, taken the advice of trusted counsellors, and weighed up all the pros and cons, the ultimate step has to be a step of faith. He can never be *completely* certain that it is the right decision, any more than the response to other vocations can bring absolute certainty for 'we walk by faith and not by sight'. We all have to make the leap of faith. But 'the assurance given by Christ in the Gospel that celibates for the Kingdom of Heaven's sake are following his example and are in communion with his manhood, and the assertions of St. Paul concerning the value of celibacy for the ministry, will be supports on which faith and decision can be solidly based.'[1]

Clearly no one should rush into celibacy. There is a need to exercise great patience in testing the call of God. Church history tells us of the over-zealous and extreme actions of men like Origen, but the work of the Kingdom is best served by a sane and balanced zeal rather than fanaticism. In considering the possibility of a vocation to celibacy, one Principal advised his theological students to 'Take your time, and be genuinely open to God in your prayer and in your life.'

[1] Ibid.

The supreme example of the celibate is to be seen in Jesus himself. From the gospel records we see quite clearly how impossible it would have been for him to have carried out his particular mission had he had family responsibilities. His need to be available to all was indicated when he asked that curious question: 'Who are my mother and my brethren?' On the surface it might have sounded like a terrible slight on his family, but surely it was an idiomatic way of saying that his mission required an unattached love of all men. There were the constant and pressing crowds, the irregular hours of work and sleep, the Son of Man with nowhere to lay his head, with no settled abode and no fixed income. There were the long nights of prayer, the trips into Gentile countries in order to give periods of concentrated teaching to his disciples, and always, from his baptism on, the knowledge that his was to be a mission of rejection and that his hour would finally come.

Celibacy brings loneliness — the same loneliness that all single people feel, but there is the added burden that the celibate is called upon to carry the sorrows and problems of many of his confidants. Just as most positions of leadership carry their special forms of loneliness, so is it true of the Christian ministry. There are some things a minister can share with no one — not even his wife. But a wife can share some of the heaviness of heart and weariness of soul without knowing any details. The celibate may not be able to share this with anyone. The ache that the celibate sometimes feels has been most powerfully expressed by Michel Quoist in his prayer, 'The Priest: a prayer on Sunday night':[1]

Tonight Lord, I am alone.
Little by little the sounds died down in the church,
The people went away,
And I came home,
Alone.
I passed people who were returning from a walk.

[1] Michel Quoist, *The Prayers of Life* (Gill & Son), p. 49.

I went by the cinema that was disgorging its crowd,
I skirted café terraces where tired strollers were trying to
  prolong the pleasure of a Sunday holiday.
I bumped into youngsters playing on the footpath,
Youngsters, Lord,
Other people's youngsters who will never be my own.
Here I am Lord,
Alone,
The silence troubles me,
The solitude oppresses me.
Lord, I'm thirty-five years old,
A body made like others,
  ready for work,
A heart meant for love,
But I've given you all.
It's true of course that you needed it.
I've given you all, but it's hard Lord.
It's hard to give one's body; it would like to give itself
  to others.
It's hard to love everyone and to claim no one.
It's hard to shake a hand and not want to retain it.
It's hard to inspire affection, to give it to you.
It's hard to be nothing to oneself in order to be everything
  to others.
It's hard to be like others, among others, and to be of them,
It's hard always to give without trying to receive,
It's hard to seek out others and to be unsought oneself.
It's hard to suffer from the sins of others, and yet be
  obliged to hear and bear them.
It's hard to be told secrets and to be unable to share them.
It's hard to carry others and never, even for a moment, be
  carried,
It's hard to sustain the feeble and never be able to lean on one
  who is strong.
It's hard to be alone,
Alone before everyone,

Alone before the world,
Alone before suffering,
  death,
  sin.

Son, you are not alone,
I am with you . . .

Lord tonight, while all is still and I feel sharply the sting of
  solitude,
While men devour my soul and I feel incapable of satisfying
  their hunger,
While the whole world presses on my shoulders with all its
  weight of misery and sin,
I repeat to you my 'yes'—not in a burst of laughter, but
  slowly, clearly, humbly,
Alone Lord, before you,
In the peace of the evening.

As we reflect on the life and ministry of Jesus, could not much
of that prayer have been his? It is true that he had the company
of his disciples, but sometimes their inability to understand him
must have increased his loneliness rather than alleviated it.
Perhaps this was one of the reasons why he withdrew for long
periods of prayer. While it may seem trite to suggest that
prayer is the answer to loneliness, in the calling of the celibate
he has this clear example of the Lord. 'In his solitude only
Christ can fill his need of love, and it is in prayer that he will
find all his joy.'[1]

There is too, for all who have renounced marriage for the
sake of the Kingdom, the promise that he will receive a
hundredfold brothers, sisters, children now in this present time.
As one Religious once said:[2]

  Chastity does not consist of deadening our heart, but

[1] *Marriage and Celibacy*, p. 111.
[2] Mother Jane Margaret of Wantage.

rather in giving it a liberty of love, a single aim, a transparency to God. Our chastity, indeed our whole life, only makes sense in relation to our love for God. True we do find Him and love Him in one another. I doubt whether I should ever have experienced such wealth and depth of love, from and for so many, had I not followed what I believed, and still believe, to be my vocation. I hesitate to speak so personally, yet at the risk of sounding presumptuous I must say this, because it sums up what I have been trying to get across. Gradually over the years there has been drawn out of me a love, an outgoing love, which I know is not my own. It is not something I have conjured up myself, nor striven for directly. It is something that has been given to me, something that has happened almost without my being aware of it. It is very real. More than that, I would say it is reality. I can only think it is something of the hundredfold promised to us by our Lord.

Natural loneliness can only really be overcome by the supernatural gifts that are given to those who respond to the vocation of celibacy. As Gilbert Russell has put it.[1]

. . . religion and sex [H. A. Williams would add 'gin and chatter'] are the two principal methods by which men and women have sought to overcome loneliness, and to still the pain of the wound of separation. 'It is not good that man should be alone.' The original man within us echoes this: he knows that it is not good for man to live alone. Body and soul affirm it. Of course a man or woman may accept this condition and even embrace it; it may be thrust upon them and they submit or rebel. But they hardly *accept* it (whether chosen or not) with its manifold possibilities of fruition and power, unless they will recognise that it lacks a 'goodness' natural to man, and that only a supernatural good can repair the loss . . .

---

[1] Gilbert Russell, *Men and Women* (S.C.M.), p. 64.

When religion and sex are regarded as *alternative* means of transcending man's isolation, both are degraded. Christianity has not escaped this danger: it has sometimes been represented as primarily a device for the *mastery* of sex, that is, the suppression of it as a 'rival'—rather than the method of its sanctification.

Psychologists sometimes talk of bachelors or spinsters as being emotionally maimed and incomplete. Sadly, there *are* those of whom this could be said, but it is not necessarily the case with all unmarrieds. Jesus has been described (as I said earlier) as the Proper Man, the only one who has ever been truly complete, with an unruffled inner harmony. We all have a 'shadow' side to our personalities. 'It seems that as we try to bring light, serve truth and do good, the opposite side grows with the same intensity. This phenomenon is so independent of our conscious intention, so difficult to face steadily and to cope with that gradually a dissociation occurs, splitting us apart.'[1] But Jesus was like the sun—all light. Could he be said to be emotionally maimed? Was he an incomplete person as a celibate?

We have already discussed (in Chapter 1) the fundamental need for completeness through the man-woman relationship. We need also to note that there is a distinction to be drawn between the polarity of male and female and the complementariness of men and women. 'The mutual relationship which God saw to be good includes the physical but transcends it . . . any attempt to reduce the mutual interdependence of men and women to a mere physical relationship, in effect destroys what God found good.'[2]

In the Old Testament, the People of God were fulfilling their purpose and obeying the will of God by being fruitful and multiplying. The rightness of the interdependence of male and female is shown by the fact that no religious sanctions were

[1] James Hillman, *Insearch* (Hodder and Stoughton), p. 62.
[2] Canadian Ecumenical Report.

necessary for marriage. Every man was expected to marry and 'what was right in the purposes of God did not require human sanctions to justify it'.

In the New Testament, however, the trend is to play down the emphasis on the mutual interdependence of male and female. 'So then, there is no difference . . . between male and female; you are all one in union with Christ Jesus' (Gal. 3:28). In some sense therefore a new order seems to have been established in which the interdependence of male and female as opposed to person and person is made, if not irrelevant, at least of diminished importance.

This shift in emphasis seems to have something to do with the person and work of Christ himself. As the Proper Man, he is the norm of the new realm, and through obedience to him and mystical union with him, each individual Christian gradually conforms more and more to His likeness. Christ in some sense transcends the traditional polarity of male and female. He is complete in himself.

> He can neither be identified satisfactorily with men as distinct from women, nor with women as distinct from men. Yet both men and women can equally identify with Him. If the man-woman polarity can be said to remain in Christ in some way, it does so within His own person, freed from its ordinary linkage with the objective differentiation of male and female.[1]

If Christ were only the Proper Man, a kind of shining example, it would be more disheartening than helpful. But he is, in one sense, the intrusion of God into the inside of human life to set it right. This creates a new situation, with new dimensions of meaning. The particular way in which Christ seems to transcend the polarity of man and woman becomes an expression of God's purposes for men. In the first creation, man accepted God's purposes for him 'by accepting the mutual

[1] Ibid.

interdependence of man and woman in its linkage with the biological sex functions'.[1] In the new creation presented through the New Testament, there seems at least a suggestion that this may not be the only path of obedience. Man may be called to fulfil God's purposes for him through by-passing or transcending in some way the man-woman polarity, or at least by dissociating it from the purely biological male-female relationship.

Man is made in the image of God the Redeemer as well as God the Creator. In order to fulfil their responsibility to share in God's redemptive activity, both men and women may be called on to transcend the reproductive aspect of male-female polarity, whether in vocations requiring celibacy or marriage.

If we are right in saying that the 'new creature in Christ' may be either male or female without biological sexuality being a major factor, we then need to ask ourselves and to seek to define, in what ways the transcendence spoken of above implies both fulfilment and negation of the sexual distinctions. What clues do we get from a study of the life of Christ? Is it possible, for instance, for the man-woman polarity to exist to some degree in a single person, and if so, did it exist in the Incarnate Christ?

We have been so conditioned to think of very clear-cut distinctions between the sexes that such a question is a difficult one. Society, traditionally, has tended to stereotype everyone as male or female, whereas modern genetical research has taught us that nature recognises a great range of intermediary types neither clearly male or female. Perhaps the arrival of the unisex is not altogether a joke. All human beings are a combination of both sexes and wholeness implies the accepting and cultivating of one's femininity (the Anima) as a man, and one's masculinity (the Animus) as a woman?

THE VOW OF CHASTITY

So far in this chapter the emphasis has been upon celibate

[1] Ibid.

clergy but all that is now said applies to all those men and women who have accepted vows of chastity (and this too is a much misunderstood term) as part of their rule, either individually or within religious orders. Sometimes people regard 'religious' as though they were people of 'weak natural affections or emotions, who have successfully disciplined those they have almost out of existence'. This, as Sister Edna Mary has said 'is, or ought to be, a complete travesty of the truth, and the distaste which it evokes is thoroughly healthy. The vow of chastity is a means by which natural love is disciplined, certainly, but the purpose and effect of the discipline is to strengthen and direct that love, not to destroy it.'[1] The late Mother Jane Margaret of Wantage, speaking on the vow of chastity, gave her own moving testimony to what it had meant to her during the forty years of her professed life. She asked:

Should not chastity be a positive dynamic way of witness in this present age of permissiveness, and sex-obsession? As I have understood it, it never was prudery, nor a cold negation of our humanity, a maiming of life. God could not call us to a maimed half existence. Don't we offer Him ourselves, our souls and bodies to be a *living* sacrifice?

We are whole people, wholly given — or rather we want to be. We can't give ourselves to God in bits and pieces. Just because we dedicate ourselves in chastity it doesn't mean that our human sexuality is going to fade out automatically, nor do we want it to do so. It is as much part of us as any other, and it can be, and is, used in other ways than the physical. If we tried to kill that side of us we should kill ourselves. And where, then, would the living sacrifice be?

But before we can be wholly whole we do need purification, and this is where pain comes in. There must be discipline in our loving — discipline which is not the same thing as repression. If we try to repress our sexuality by refusing or fearing to face and accept it, it will only break out in ugly

[1] Sister Edna Mary, *The Religious Life* (Penguin), p. 153.

9

ways such as jealousy, moodiness, withdrawal, which can all be unconscious cries for the satisfaction of our natural desires. And this is sad because these things make us lesser people than we ought to be. Chastity is not meant to stunt our personality. . . .

Many of the great saints, though celibate, were people of very strong affections which if 'undisciplined, would have smothered the persons loved', but disciplined, could become the basis for an intense devotion towards God, rich relationships with other people and immense compassion for those in great need. They were people with a great appetite for life and an enormous capacity for love who, by putting it at the service and disposal of God, found that the capacity was in fact strengthened and not repressed. A Jesuit once said: 'Chastity is not a curtailment of the power to love but a concentration of that power.' In his book *The New Nuns* Michael Novak describes how these sisters in America have channelled their natural love in such a wholesome way that one catches as one reads something of their warmth. He says that a nun is someone who has chosen to make herself available to all as a sister rather than as a wife and mother. Many who enter religious orders are far from cool and detached people with under-developed affections. They are more often those whose 'temperament would be likely to lead them to love with more fervour than wisdom, who need discipline to harness this capacity for love so that it may be fruitful in the service of God'.[1]

One of the particular joys of the celibate is that he or she is free to love deeply without fear of misunderstanding. It is obviously possible that misunderstandings can arise for any kind of loving carries its own particular risks within it. But at least the celibate has openly declared his position and, in his relationships with people of the opposite sex, he need not feel that he is irresponsibly arousing marriage expectations which he

[1] Sister Edna Mary, *The Religious Life.*

cannot fulfil. It is possible for two people who have both accepted the gift of celibacy, to love each other with an astonishing depth, to discover that the transcending of the male-female polarity in their relationship is not just a fond ideal but a reality. There can be immense freedom and openness in a friendship where both know that marriage does not enter into the picture at all.

Fr. Gerald Vann has given a superb illustration of this in *To Heaven with Diana*[1] which is a study of the love of Jordan of Saxony for Diana d'Andale. Jordan was head of the Dominican Order and Diana founded the contemplative branch of the Dominicans. Here were two celibates who knew an extraordinarily strong bond of mutual love. In the correspondence between them, it is quite clear that Diana's love for Jordan deepens and strengthens his love for her. Although Jordan was giving Diana a great deal of help, she was equally helping him. 'That is why they are in effect such a wonderful treatise on Christian friendship.'

This kind of loving not only gives a man more love for other men, but also more love for God. Of course there are dangers in such a love—especially the danger of becoming too absorbed in one another to the neglect of essential duties, 'but danger is not the same as disaster'. Jordan, expounding on the parable of the talents and the man who hid his talent in a napkin, says:

What of the idea of vocation which means using for God the gifts that God has given you? You must be constant, gay, prudent; and of course where danger is greater, there prudence must be greater too . . . At the bar of heaven we shall be expected only to say how we have done with our fasting and alms and deeds and pursuits of virtue . . . and we shall not, still more, be expected to say: 'You gave me though unworthy, the love of these your children to keep me gay in heart to help me in the dark places, and I tried to be prudent and let no harm come thereby to them or to me.' We must

[1] Fr. Gerald Vann, *To Heaven with Diana* (Collins).

also say: 'but also I tried not to disparage the gift nor refuse its responsibilities.' If, in other words, you grow more and more free of egoism, rapacity and greed, then you have less and less cause for fear: you can find a better motive in all that you do than the cult of safety.

One of the problems about celibacy is that too often it has been regarded as a virtue in itself, rather than as part of a particular vocation. The idea of renunciation and sacrifice has been so over-emphasised that the truth about the gift in this vocation has been ignored. This can lead to a false sense of superiority. Dr. Leonard Hodgson has rightly drawn attention to our tendency to make unfavourable comparisons with those whose walks of life differ from our own.[1]

> Life is not long enough for each of us to give full expression to all his many selves. The love which is to unify them has therefore to take the form of recognising the value of those which cannot be indulged. They are not to be suppressed or repressed as evil; they are to be offered in willing surrender to God because He wills us to give precedence to some other self as the centre of the particular work that he has for us to do on earth. The man who is called to be a scholar must curb his desire to engage in manifold practical activities. If, for a while, he has to go and be soldier, he must put aside his civilian pursuits. If he is called to work in which marriage is impossible, he must be continent with good grace. But he will only do any of these things with a good grace if he maintains a gracious attitude towards the selves he cannot satisfy, if he avoids the temptation to seal up the doors of his mind against the interests he cannot pursue and lets a love for them fertilise and enrich, without distracting, the self which is to be the centre of his life.

This graciousness cannot be achieved by man except by the grace of God. Our natural pride makes us disinclined to

[1] Leonard Hodgson, *Doctrine of the Trinity* (Nisbet), p. 3.

acknowledge that we are finite beings who cannot foster all kinds of good; it inclines us to justify our self-limitation by holding that we have chosen what is better and renounced what is worse. So long as we are trusting in our own strength, our natural weakness requires us to buttress our self-denial by building up a sentiment of reprobation or scorn towards the interests we have renounced. Thus the achievement of a false unity in our lives makes us incapable of taking a further step in graciousness, and appreciating the contributions which others can make to human life, just because they are different from our own. It may be that they are called to put in the centre selves which we have to put on one side. It may be that they can express selves which we do not seem to have in us at all, which may indeed even be uncongenial to our tastes.

The celibate must neither covet the married man, nor consider himself superior to him. Both have been obedient in accepting their different vocations to express a particular 'self'. Both are vocations to love. God has given to each his gift, and therefore there are absolutely no grounds for boasting or pride. The only response to the gift in either case is a humble acceptance and worthy use of it.

CHAPTER SEVEN

The Question of Choice

IN ALMOST ANY AREA OF LIFE YOU CAN MAKE A CHOICE AND follow it through. One of the frustrating things about marriage is that you have very little *choice* in the matter! There are some highly attractive people who seem to have a succession of suitors or girl friends from whom they can make a choice. It is perfectly normal for young people to date, or even court, several friends before choosing *the one*.

For women, it is the case that (whatever their inner longings for a partner and family may be), they cannot actually choose but must be chosen. This produces a sense of helplessness. However much they encourage, prompt or use their feminine artistry, ultimately the initiative must come from the man. That certainly has been the cultural pattern up till now. We have yet to see what changes Women's Lib will bring about, but let us hope that, whatever they may be, women will not rob men of their maleness, their role as protectors and providers as well as lovers. However, Women's Lib does not carry the wholehearted sympathy of all women, as Marjorie Holmes makes clear in this prayer:

Lord help us to realise our mistakes and get back into balance. Men and women are not the same. You didn't make us so, you didn't mean us to be.

You gave men strengths and skills and differences no woman can match. And you made women different, blessedly, wonderfully different from men.

Lord please help us to find our true identity and self expression without hurting, humbling, emasculating and making enemies of our men.[1]

Even if we think that it is desirable that the proposal should come from the man and even if we have no wish to change this pattern, it does not remove a certain feeling of helplessness if you long for marriage but see no prospect of those longings being fulfilled. You may hope and pray and wait, then, as the years pass, you may find fulfilment in some other channel of loving and accept singleness even quite gladly. This is fine and good, but one has come to that point through acceptance rather than choice.

A man, having the initiative, probably does not feel the same helplessness and frustration, though he may feel miserably inadequate if he finds it difficult to relate closely to women. We tend to think that all bachelors are so by choice, but for some, the longings may be just as acute as they are for women.

We may not be able to choose to marry but we *do* have freedom to choose *not* to marry. This point brings us to a form of voluntary renunciation that has not yet been covered, namely marriage set aside for the sake of a career. There are some men who feel that the conflict of family loyalties and home duties would tie them down and impede their progress in their chosen profession. This is not on the whole a major problem for a man. The fact that he is cared for by a wife and family can in fact release him to give more energy to his work.

For the woman it is different, or at least has been different traditionally. The career woman may choose to remain single because she feels that, for her, married life and the natural longings to put her time and energy into the home and domestic pursuits would create an inner conflict. To 'get on' in her

[1] M. Holmes, *Who Am I God?* (Hodder and Stoughton), p. 68.

career she may need freedom to travel, to be out frequently in the evenings, to have a fairly full social life, to bring papers home and work late into the night . . . none of which would be easy for a husband to accept or tolerate indefinitely. The biggest problem of all obviously is the possible interruption of her work in the event of a pregnancy and the need to care for her children.

You cannot tell whether a woman has thrown herself into her career because that is her first love or because, not being married, it satisfies a need. It is difficult even to know the true motivation in oneself let alone in others, but there are women who firmly declare that they have turned down marriage because it would interfere with their career prospects.

That is a legitimate choice and often the right one, a fact demonstrated by the tremendous service they render through their work. But one sometimes fears a little for them. It is so very easy to become wrongly ambitious. A certain amount of ambition and drive is thoroughly healthy, but, beyond a particular point, it becomes threatening because it can sweep other people aside or even steam-roller them in its onrush. In some spheres you *can* only succeed if you enter the rat race with all its competitive spirit. This can quickly lead to hardness in both men and women. A woman in the power game needs to exercise immense caution for it would be so easy to settle for a way of life that fails to make the special contribution her femininity has to offer.

Those who *choose* to walk alone need to beware of one thing more. It is a warning that needs to be stressed again and again to all single people. There is, perhaps, a special danger for the 'career men and women'. If, in any way, they are 'hardening', it will begin to show in their life style. They will probably grow more selfish and may want to isolate themselves more from their families. It is alarming how selfishness can thrive unwittingly when you walk alone.

This does not mean that all successful people are wildly

ambitious, hardened, selfish and unfeeling towards their parents. They are not. It is only a warning that the danger is there in a more acute form than for most other single people.

There are other walks of life where people may not necessarily have renounced marriage, but in following that way they have wittingly accepted a severe limitation to their chances of marrying. Whenever you are cut off from normal contacts with the opposite sex, you are inevitably reducing the possibilities of meeting a life partner. Perhaps the most obvious example of this is, for a man, the lonely explorer whose travels sometimes prevent him from committing himself to any degree of permanence in a relationship. We may be coming to a time when those who wish to be involved in space exploration will see singleness as preferable to marriage.

Missionary life imposes similar limitations. It is not that missionary societies require candidates to be single, but if you go out to serve in a lonely part of the world, then it often means (for a woman at any rate) that the only men you will meet will be married men. This is not the whole picture, of course. Many single men and women have met in their 'adopted' country, and have fallen in love and married as a result. But there does seem to be a preponderance of single women in the field and, where there are no eligible men around at all, then there is no choice *but* to remain single. Recognising what it would mean to be sent to a lonely bush station or to a small island in the Pacific with mail boats arriving only once every three months, we used to repeat a little rhyme when we were students in missionary training:

I'm a little celibate 'mish'
Sublimating every wish.
Nobody put me on the shelf
'Cos I climbed up there by myself!
(But just sometimes I come down for dusting!!)

There may be a tacit acceptance of singleness amongst such women missionaries, but sometimes it is even harder to bear in the conditions on the field than it would be at home. There is at times an *awful* loneliness. Cut off from so many of your friends, relations and interests in the home country, the inner loneliness that most single people feel at times, is intensified. Not surprisingly, so are your longings for a husband. Often when the work is really hard, disappointing and disheartening you long for close physical comfort, but these longings cannot be met because male colleagues are all married, because you would not want comfort expressed in quite that way by another woman, and because there can be tremendous complications if you enter into that kind of close bond with one of the men nationals. Added to all this, many of us found that tropical heat increased normal sexual desire which was all the harder to cope with in a society where singleness was virtually unknown.

At the time when I was working in the Congo (now Zaire) single women missionaries were accepted and loved but always regarded as something of freaks. Some of my students actually asked a married colleague what dreadful thing it was that I had done in England that necessitated my father shipping me off to Africa! On another station where there was one married couple and three single women, it was firmly held that all four women were 'wives' of the male missionary but that his (actual) wife was just his No. 1 and favourite wife. To work in a society that neither understood singleness, nor appreciated that in order to work in remote foreign parts, one gave up many chances of marriage, but which at the same time had a strong emphasis upon sex and family life (all the while coping with heightened sexual longings) was by no means easy. When we valedict young missionaries, it would be well to remember that there are many costs in such a life and this may be one of them.

A much bigger group of people who have made sacrifices where marriage prospects are concerned, is that of the single men and women who have dependent parents or other family responsibilities. More often than not they begin with the expectation of marriage and a home of their own but the years of the twenties and early thirties slip quickly by. They have not left home. In fact, far from leaving home, they have begun to shoulder more and more of the burdens of the house and its running. Parents may be growing weaker and therefore more dependent and it may dawn, quite suddenly, on the single person that it would be almost impossible to extricate themselves from this situation. If a possible partner came along, it would be so painful and difficult to leave home and the ageing parents who have learned to lean (hard sometimes) on their single son or daughter, marriage would be out of the question.

More often than not however, there is no danger of a possible partner looming up on the horizon because the single person is rarely free to go out and mix with contemporaries in any social context. It is well to recognise that some of them are tremendously tied by ageing parents, and sometimes *so* tied that it presents real financial difficulties.

Single women who look after aged and infirm relatives with no financial support constitute one of London's (and, presumably, other cities') growing social problems. It is to help such women that the National Council for the Single Woman and her Dependants (166, Victoria Street, S.W.1, and registered in 1965) was formed. Speaking of a campaign to persuade local authorities to provide sites for housing schemes, with wardens, for the women and their families so that single women catering for dependants could continue to work and thus augment the meagre family budget, the director of the Council said:

Our research shows that many of these women are living below the poverty line having had to give up work to care for their parents.

Very often they are not even able to get a holiday or an evening out. Many have sacrificed the prospect of marriage and a family of their own to do what they consider to be their duty.

Pressure on the Government succeeded in getting an attendance allowance of (originally) £4·80 per week for old people who are infirm and have to stay at home. But this only applies if the elderly person is sick. What is needed is more help for single people looking after parents and elderly relatives who are only really suffering from the normal old-age symptoms. Once single women have given up their jobs to nurse the elderly, they can quickly become completely tied to that responsibility.

As one woman said, having given up her work at a college after twenty one years there: ' . . . I have no time at all to myself except when I can arrange for my sister to come and sit in. I am completely tied to the home. But what is the alternative? It's either a geriatric ward in hospital or paying £40 a week for a place in a nursing home. I don't want one and I can't afford the other.'

Another woman who was similarly tied said: 'Only those who have been through this particular hell alone know what a toll it takes both physically and mentally, to say nothing about financially.'

Another said: 'Do you know anyone who could come and look after my father while I go on holiday? I can carry on, but only if I have a break.'

These sort of pleas could be echoed over and over again from countless other single women. There is little hope of their forming new friendships in these circumstances, let alone courting.

Many single people would however, be quite uncomplaining about the burden of responsibility in itself. What *is* hard to bear is the cool assumption on the part of other (usually married) members of the family that:

' . . . of course X will look after mother or father, or both. After all, she's single.'

When her elderly mother became rather too old to live alone, a single woman missionary friend of mine was expected by the rest of the family to give up her life and calling in Africa (which had become home for her) and return to England to care for her mother. There were three other sisters and a brother in this country, but the 'obvious' solution was to get the single daughter back to live at home. It was a solution, certainly, but not necessarily obvious!

There is a head teacher who has to rush home at weekends and in the holidays to look after her nearly blind mother and deal with any matters needing attention in the house. However much she would like to relax in her own flat, she has to make the long journey to her mother regularly. Yet her brother and his family live less than five minutes' walk away.

The other members of such families often tend to argue, 'Well, she has no family of her own to consider — it's easier for her to move than those of us with children.' 'Easier' — Yes. But for whom? It is by no means easy for the single son or daughter to give up a flat or house, their independence and free social life, maybe even their jobs. Yet it often seems to fall to them to do so. What of the sacrifices to the single son or daughter? They may have longed for a family of their own. Now the fact that they haven't one, is flung back at them as grounds for giving up what independence they have.

You cannot of course, generalise on this subject. It is certainly not true of all families, and most single people would, in any case, recognise that they do have particular responsibilities in these situations. But any renunciation must be voluntary, not because it is expected of them. It is easy enough to advise single people not to be 'put upon', and correspondingly difficult to carry out such advice. Where care of parents is necessary, the happiest thing is to accept it as the responsibility of the *whole* family, not just of the single son or daughter.

If the son or daughter is an only child it is a different matter. He or she may realise that there is no choice but to look after the parents and will gladly accept the responsibility. But, in that case, would it not be a good thing to keep a measure of freedom? For example, it would help to have a separate sitting room for entertaining and for privacy. One bachelor I know has a room furnished as his music room where he can entertain those friends who are music lovers. If there can be clearly agreed times when the son or daughter can go out and a 'sitter' comes in, it prevents that feeling of being utterly tied.

If possible ensure that you have agreed times when the parent(s) go out, or, if that is not practicable, when visitors come. Perhaps it would be possible to arrange a rota of friends and neighbours. Many churches these days have a system of baby-sitters to enable young married couples to get out together. What an immense help it would be if more of them organised a similar system of 'sitters' for aged parents.

Wherever possible, it is sensible to have help in the house. If at work all day, the single person should not have to toil every evening on household chores. Unfortunately however, one has to be realistic and see that there are financial restrictions that put such help right out of the reach of some.

One word of caution to single women in this situation is needed. Try not to become *wholly* absorbed in Mother and Father and the house. There is a big, wide world outside that needs you too. Perhaps that sounds presumptuous coming from one who can only advise as an onlooker, but it is offered lovingly. While this book seeks to deal as comprehensively as possible with the question of singleness, it would be impossible for an author to have run the whole gamut of what can be involved in 'walking alone' and I, myself, have not had to cope with this problem personally. I have, however, met quite a number of middle-aged spinster daughters who look far older than their years because they rarely ever mix with younger company. Their lives have become narrowly circumscribed because they never see beyond the needs of their own small family unit. Their whole lives are devoted to, and wrapped up in, their parents—which is not always as admirable as we may suppose it to be. Sometimes the knowledge that they are needed, that their parents lean upon them and look to them as protectors is a way of fulfilling their own needs; or, it can become so. When this happens, the death of the parents brings not only the normal sense of loss and grief, but a quite awful feeling of personal deprivation, and possibly even clinical depression.

Single people owe it to themselves to have some independent life and interests. They need to look ahead and prepare for the time when they will not have Mother and/or Father to care for. For some sons, but more particularly daughters, the bottom of their world drops out when both parents die. Not only do they feel they have lost their *raison d'être*, but they are often faced with appalling loneliness. During the time they have cared for their parents, they may not have kept up with their friends and the friendships have died of atrophy. Sometimes they have lost touch with or the taste for social activities.

As the National Council for the Single Woman and her Dependants discovered: 'For many, the real loneliness starts after their parents have died, and they find themselves on their own—cut off from society and friends.'

Somehow a way must be found round the problem of having time for friends. We all need friends and grow in maturity through them. Surely it would be wrong to be so self-effacing, so self-sacrificing that one does not grow oneself into the richness and joy of maturity? An article called 'The Quest of Secular Obedience' states:[1]

> The idea that any unmarried person may, and indeed must, like married people, achieve an independent personal life, is not self-evident to many parents, nor indeed to some unmarried people themselves. The terms 'bachelor' and 'spinster' often designate those whom marriage has not freed from parental control. The spinster, for example, will, unless she is careful, be marked out for all the additional tasks her relatives can find for her.

[1] Published in *The Way* by the English Jesuits.

It is true that unmarried people do bear heavy responsibility for their parents and family. An unmarried son or daughter is, after all, more free than the married to help aged parents in distress. There are, therefore, certain family obligations which may not be evaded under the pretext of secular consecration. But to be sure that such obligations are really genuine, really grounded in a human situation and in harmony with the will of God, calls for the gifts of clear thinking and discernment. These in turn will require complete freedom from attitudes of dependence proper to children, but which have nothing to do with human maturity and Christian freedom. Thus the unmarried person should try to acquire as soon as possible a genuine freedom with regard to lodging, use of time, friends, leisure activities, comings and goings. Without standing on principle but with a quiet resolution and as much tact and discretion as possible, the unmarried person must bring his family to accept the way in which his own personal liberty expresses itself.

One single woman with a dependent, aged mother seems to have found a positive solution. She has a residential post and her mother lives with her. It was a situation that had much potential for irritation and mutual chafing, instead of which their flat radiates joy. The daughter shares as much of her work as she can with her mother, bringing home to tea needy and lonely people. They talk over such friends, together they pray for them, plan for them and keep an open house so that although the mother is unable to get out, she is fully active in a joint ministry with her daughter. The daughter, of course, is very fortunate to have a mother who *can* so share. It would not be so with all single people.

There are three other areas where we might regard people as restricted in their choice or in their likelihood of being chosen for marriage.

It is not true to say that physically handicapped people have no choice. There have been some triumphant stories of marriages from wheelchairs, marriages of armless and legless people, polio victims and so on. They have discovered that their disabilities did not bar the way finally to marriage.

One such woman told how, all through her teens it had been impressed upon her that she *could never* marry. It was probably with the most loving intent that her parents so tried to prepare her for what they assumed must be inevitable. Then, at a day centre for the physically handicapped, she met and fell in love with another handicapped person. They determined to marry against all the advice of friends, and with a purpose built ground floor flat, their two wheel chairs and invalid carriages, they are not only able to cope but are blissfully happy.

That is one of many such stories. Nevertheless, for many other young people with a physical handicap, it must be a question that lurks constantly in the back of the mind. Does this rule out marriage for me? The choice is undoubtedly a diminished one and we need to remember with real sensitivity that for all such, there can be moments of bitter realisation.

Until fairly recently, it was assumed that mentally handicapped people would not and should not marry. To what extent then do the mentally handicapped have any choice in the matter of marriage? Clearly there are some forms of mental handicap that would make marriage and the possibility of a family wholly inappropriate. Many thus handicapped are legally within their rights to marry after the age of sixteen, but the question scarcely arises for them. Their choice is minimal yet their need of love and companionship is as great if not greater than those so-called 'normal' people. How far is their need to relate closely to one other person considered in their overall care? How far would a close relationship help towards fuller integration? These are questions which the medical experts alone can answer, but they are questions we need to think about if we are to be adequately sympathetic in this realm of freedom to choose.

The third area of handicap is a religious one. The choices

10

in marriage are limited for those deeply committed to a faith. Probably there are Moslem, Hindu and Buddhist young people in our multi-racial society who are facing grave tensions in this matter. This is perhaps a newer problem that has risen in our midst. We have long lived with the problem of mixed marriages between Jews and Christians, Catholics and Protestants, Christians and other faiths or none, but now the problem is more complex. For growing up side by side in our schools are children of many different nationalities and different religious allegiances. What is happening as they grow into their teens and twenties? We encourage them in schools to recognise no racial or colour barriers. Are they then, when they come of marriageable age, to reverse some of this thinking and insist on religious loyalties? There are many reasons why one would want to say 'Yes' and yet at the same time it is a tenuous position to hold.

I am not going to attempt to answer this problem as it lies outside the scope of this book, but draw attention to these increasing difficulties in order to point out that the question of choice for some young people is going to be fraught with great and painful complications.

CHAPTER EIGHT

The Ministry of Children

WE ALL NEED CHILDREN WHETHER WE ARE SINGLE OR MARRIED of whatever age. We need children to bring us back from our sophistication to the real values of life. When we have grown weary of the rounds of office dinners and cocktail parties, the frivolous, inconsequential chatter and expensive dressing up, it is good to share a child's excitement in buying an ice cream or going to the zoo. When we have toured miles of beautiful countryside in our expensive cars, it is refreshing to see the look of awe and wonder in a child's eye as he looks at a moth or an earthworm. When we have grown so used to the good things of life that we take them all for granted, it is lovely to see the joy registering on the face of a child as he sees them for the first time.

It is good to know that there was a time when *we* could be affected like that. Once, *we* were overjoyed with simple pleasures. In our complicated, diversified ways of life, children bring us back to simplicity. We do need children, and those who are childlike in heart, as Michel Quoist has reminded us so poignantly!

God says, I like youngsters. I want people to be like them.
  I don't like old people unless they are still children.
I want only children in my Kingdom; this has been decreed
  from the beginning of time.

Youngsters—twisted, humped, wrinkled, white-bearded—all
   kinds of youngsters, but youngsters.
There is no changing it, it has been decided, there is room for
   no one else.
I like little children because my likeness has not yet been
   dulled in them.
They have not botched my likeness, they are new, pure,
   without a blot, without a smear.
But above all, I like youngsters because of the look in their
   eyes.
In their eyes I can read their age.
In my heaven, there will be only five-year-olds, for I know of
   nothing more beautiful than the pure eyes of a child ...
Hurry! Now is the time. I am ready to give you again the
   beautiful face of a child, the beautiful eyes of a child ...
For I love youngsters, and I want everyone to be like them.[1]

The unselfconsciousness and directness (it is always sad to
meet a devious child) and simple acceptance of children can
often minister to adult wounds. How often a bereaved person
has found comfort in the presence of a child who is neither
embarrassed nor afraid to ask questions, nor particularly
surprised at tears. They continue to talk freely, unless they are
restrained. They are not afraid to look straight into the eyes of
another. Their very acceptance of adult grief is a help. The idea
that an adult should never weep in front of a child is nonsense.
They can cope more readily with tears than many grown-ups
can.

Children have the power to bring out in us an innocence and
simple joy that we thought completely lost. More often than
not it has lain buried beneath the hard crust of sophistication
and sin. Somehow they can draw it out as something fresh and
green and still growing.

A young woman who had faced just about every problem a

[1] Michel Quoist, 'God says, I like youngsters' in *Prayers of Life* (Gill & Son, Logos
Books), 1967.

young woman can face in our contemporary society, was eventually rescued through the sheer love and caring of members of a city church. One day she was playing on the vicarage lawn with the vicar's children. From his study window together with a friend, the vicar stood watching her. 'Isn't she beautiful?' he said. Looking at him in some surprise, the friend saw on his face a look of utterly transparent sincerity and love. Turning back to the scene in the garden, the friend could only agree. Through the complete trust and acceptance of the children, the haggard look and tragic expression had given place to a freshness and innocence that was indeed beautiful, and through them she was recovering something of the child in herself. They were 'restoring her soul'.

In times of sorrow and degradation, children can minister to us as no adult can. But they have a ministry too in meeting people's loneliness. This was not an uncommon theme in nineteenth-century English literature as *Silas Marner* and *The Old Curiosity Shop* remind us. In a more contemporary situation it was interesting to discover in the course of organising a school's Social Service activities, that the younger members of the school made more acceptable visitors to the elderly shut-ins than did the senior pupils. The juniors were usually unselfconscious and chattered freely and easily. The old people looked forward eagerly to their regular visits.

Children can have a mellowing effect upon the most hardened grown ups. Little ones have the knack of winning their way into the hearts of the most withdrawn and unsociable people. This is particularly so where they have secure backgrounds of love and acceptance. It does not occur to them that they might not be wanted.

The story is told of a fairly gloomy, crusty, bachelor dean. One day a little girl wandered into his vestry after the morning service, perched herself prettily on the edge of a chair and began to chatter to him in the most natural and unselfconscious way. He was intrigued and touched by her complete ease with him, her direct questions and matter-of-fact comments. She did not seem in the least daunted by the fact that he was the dean. As she slipped off her chair to go, he assured her that she would be welcome to come and have another chat at any time. Her visits to the vestry after morning service became a regular thing and soon the dean began to look forward to her visits and he and the child formed a remarkable friendship which softened and warmed him. It lasted throughout her adolescent years and he continued to write to her and she to visit him even after she grew up and married.

This incident illustrates two points. First, children are sometimes less worried by positions of importance than adults. This little girl certainly wasn't awe-struck or overwhelmed! Nor was a small five-year-old boy from Stepney who stopped a former bishop of London in the course of a solemn procession round the streets and complained, 'My bruvver here (pointing to a sheepish six-year-old brother) says that Jesus *didn't* rise from the dead. It's not true, is it?' Whereupon the procession was called to a halt whilst the bishop attempted to settle the theological dispute of two East End youngsters!

The other point it illustrates is one that is often overlooked. Most people recognise that women need children in their lives and acknowledge that single women must find outlets for their maternal instincts. Not all recognise that single men need children too. The little girl in the story above did something for the dean that no adult could do. A man needs outlets for his paternal instincts. Sometimes he may feel shy and awkward with children but that is all the more reason for meeting them. He needs the kind of fulfilment that comes from a child's trust and dependence. If he *has* grown crusty or hard in any way, it will soften him to have a little hand slipped into his as a diminutive figure skips alongside him. In no time a child can hack through a bachelor's awkwardness and stiffness by clambering on to his knee and making one or two devastatingly frank observations.

Some single men are beloved of children. One bishop,

although denied a family by reason of his vow of celibacy, nevertheless creates a real family atmosphere in his home by opening it for children of the neighbourhood to drop in and watch television. He is a real friend to children and has established a close relationship with some of them. He loves to remember them on their birthdays and at Christmas and takes them out to the pantomime and sporting events. Obviously the children enjoy it enormously as the following extract from a letter shows.

Once the Bishop invited a group of children out—I was included in this. He came at about 10 a.m. in a chauffeur-driven car. He didn't show any proudness because of this, nor did he look down on his chauffeur but just laughed and joked with him, as if he was his best friend and he talked to me in the same way. He always seems to be on the same wavelength. As we were going through the town to pick up Robert, Stephen and another girl who I don't remember the name of (we nicknamed her gramophone for obvious reasons!), he asked questions about things at home and school and told me what was going to happen during the day. With the Bishop I felt quite at home. I didn't feel out of place because he was a Bishop, in fact he ignores the fact that he is a Bishop when I'm speaking to him.

When we were at the show, he stocked us up with sweets and made sure that we were all happy before he settled down, and we could not help enjoying ourselves.

Children have a delightful way of getting us to 'let down our hair'. They help us to drop airs and graces, and the worries of responsibility, and discover the child in ourselves again. You can tell quite a bit about people by the way children react to them. They will cut through all sham, hypocrisy and senti-mentality with penetrating insight, like the little boy who, in reply to an inquiry from a very gushing but unpopular aunt, said: 'Why do you always smile with your mouth when your eyes never do?' Besides 'seeing through' pretence however, they can detect hidden qualities of tenderness and humour. Have you ever seen children drawn to someone who has no sense of humour?

That great missionary figure, Temple Gairdner, was an incorrigible baby worshipper and children were drawn to him as bees to a honey pot. During his days as a travelling Secretary for the Student Christian Movement, he made the home of Colonel Oldham the base for his London operations. 'Gairdie's' comings and goings were a longed-for joy to the youngest child of the house (later to become the Rev. J. E. Oldham).

I was rather a shy and solitary small boy. But busy as he was with his work as Travelling Secretary, 'Gairdie' always seemed to have time to devote to me. After dinner he would take his seat on the piano stool and go through a series of old favourites ... I had to occupy a particular chair close to the piano in order to be directly addressed at the climax of the narrative; often I was in convulsions.

Then there were our games together. I was very keen on soldiers and 'Gairdie' would enter into the campaign most realistically, and suggested a helpful device for moving detachments about on bits of cardboard instead of man by man. One day stands out unique—two cousins, a boy and a girl a few years younger than I, were playing with me our pet game of a journey by coach, when Gairdner looked in. I can see him still, with towel draped on his head, as old 'Aunt Jane' an imaginary personage encountered on our travels ... [1]

Or there was the time when he was staying at the home of friends in Birmingham while he wrote his book on St. John. His hostess describes how 'he would spring up instantly from his meditations at the entrance of her little niece and plunge

[1] Constance Padwick, *Temple Gairdner of Cairo*, pp. 57-58.

into acting stories or songs with the child. It was, I thought, like having St. Francis or Ugo Bassi staying in the house'.[1]

Our Lord himself attracted children. Undoubtedly it was partly due to his tender heart and kindness but also, surely, because of his sense of fun? Was not his reference to children playing at weddings and funerals in the market place an indication that he must have watched a group of youngsters at play fairly recently? 'They brought young children to Him...' They would not have done that if children had not liked him. Obviously he had a wonderful rapport with them.

In order to know a person truly, you need to see them with children. Perhaps this is touchingly true of men. A church-goer once commented that she found the parson a rather fear-some character. 'He is so harsh and severe', she said. 'But, have you ever seen him with his children?' her friend asked. No, she had not. She had not seen the homely man who as a father, away from the responsibility of the church and the need to fill a particular role, was more gentle and softhearted than most women.

Sometimes an extraordinary affinity is formed between an adult and a child. A mysterious bond seems to draw them and hold them in a relationship of a special quality. Such a rela-tionship is described by Elizabeth Goudge in *Green Dolphin Country*. After an incredible escapade of climbing up some dis-used steps in the rock face, little Marguerite arrived at the Convent of Notre-Dame du Castel. There her patient knocking at the outside door of the Chapel was finally heard, and an alarmed nun admitted her. Taken to the Reverend Mother she sat drying herself before the fire in the Superior's room while she was questioned about her adventure. Her matter-of-factness and apparent unconcern about the worry she would have caused her parents seemed at first to be inconsiderate nonchalance, but the Reverend Mother soon realised her mistake.

[1] Ibid.

No, not a heartless child but one of those sensible people who do not agitate themselves when agitation can serve no useful purpose. Her whole heart had gone out to this child. She liked her courage, her honesty, her good sense, and some quality that she felt was best described by the word clarity. The sensitive nun felt this quality as the child's particular atmosphere. It seemed to beautify what she looked on not merely for herself but for others. Because of the presence of the child, Reverend Mother found herself delighting afresh in the orange glow of the firelight upon her austere white walls, and noting, as though she had not seen it before, the beauty of the old Spanish Crucifix that had companioned her through all her years of prayer. Such a gift of kindling awareness in others spoke of a spiritual strength unusual in so young a child. And she was so simple, so happy.

When her parents had been contacted and 'Papa' was at the door with the carriage, Marguerite said:

'Perhaps I shall never see you again.'

'I should be sorry not to meet you again,' said Reverend Mother and she got up and came to stand beside the child at her desk . . .

'Don't forget me,' she said, 'for I am your friend. And don't forget Notre-Dame du Castel or where it is that we find our special Country.'

'No, I won't forget,' said Marguerite, and she stood with her head lifted, her hands behind her back, looking up into the face of the tall nun. They did not kiss each other, for Reverend Mother had no use for kisses but their eyes met with the unflinching look of those who face a parting with full determination to meet again if possible.[1]

OUR ROLES WITH THE CHILDREN

How then may children minister to us and we to them if we

[1] Elizabeth Goudge, *Green Dolphin Country* (Hodder and Stoughton), pp. 93-94.

don't happen to have little girls wandering into our studies, or scrambling up cliffs to land on our doorsteps? What if we do not seem to have special affinities or special drawing powers? How may we feel a sense of belonging to a child if it is not possible to leave our front door open for the children of the neighbourhood to pour in? What roles are open to the single man or woman?

The most obvious contact is probably with nieces, nephews, and god-children. Most of us have actual nieces and nephews, and many of us have a fair number of 'adopted' ones. To be a favourite (or perhaps more accurately a favoured) aunt or uncle is a wonderful privilege and a great joy. To be a god-parent, in the true sense of the word, is a tremendous responsibility and brings (or could bring) one into an even closer bond with a child than being an aunt or uncle. For the god-parent has been asked by the parents to take a solemn share in the nurture and spiritual growth of their child. He is *chosen* for the particular qualities the parents admire in him and the esteem in which they hold him. Whereas to be an aunt or uncle is settled by the matter of blood ties.

To be an aunt, uncle or god-parent not only brings us into contact with a child and provides outlets for our maternalism or paternalism. It gives us a vested interest in the future. The father of two young children described how, at the birth of his children, he felt a continuity not only with the past but with the future too. He now cared more about the future of the country — the politics and education, housing and employment conditions — because he had a stake in it. He was linked as strongly to the future as he was undeniably to the past. Our responsibilities as single people to those children who have been brought into the circle of our love and care, give us too a real concern about the future — *their* future. We may not be able to perpetuate our own flesh and blood in offspring, but as part of the human family we have huge responsibilities about the kind of world we are building, and our distinct contribution matters. Possibly the younger countries have much to teach us here where the accent is on the *family as a whole* rather than on the Mother-Father-Child unit. Everyone in the family has a responsibility and share in the upbringing of the children. While this may be easier to practise in an African village where the family is largely together, nevertheless it speaks to us of a community concept which may be of far reaching importance.

Sometimes as a friend of the family, one can be the 'confidant' of the children. One single woman asked a married couple (who were great friends of hers) how they saw her contribution in the family relationship. They answered:

First of all, there is a particular contribution to the children. It is important that they know *well* adults who are not actual relatives but who can be 'senior friends', who follow each stage of the child's development. We feel that if ever either of our two daughters found it difficult to turn to us as parents for help, then, because of the mutual relationship that we have fostered, they will be free to confide in you. And we shall not resent this if we have, amongst the three of us, an honest and loving relationship.

Second, you have a contribution to make to us. When so often her days are taken up with the shopping and the home, Lucy [the wife] feels you can help her to think, by bringing her bits of your world and by acting as a sounding board for her. That goes for me too (said the husband) when we have time to sit and talk. We find it a help to discuss with you our hopes and fears for the children, as well as the more technical matters such as which 'O' levels might be useful.

The single woman went on to say that, for *her*, it was important to be able to discuss the relationship openly and frankly. Even if a single woman *knows* that she is welcome to her married friends, and is the trusted confidant of their children, there are times when this probably needs to be spelled out. When such reassurance is verbalised (maybe even demonstrated) within the right context of openness and love, the single woman can bear the slightly different flow of her love because she knows that the mainstream is the same for all three.

Those called into the ministry of the Church have unique opportunities for channelling their fatherly care in their love for their spiritual children. As far as we know St. Paul had no natural children, but his letters are full of a deep and loving concern for his spiritual offspring. To the Galatians he wrote: 'Oh my children, how you are hurting me! I am once again suffering for you the pains of a mother waiting for her child to be born . . . ' (Gal. 4:19). To the Thessalonians he wrote: '. . . we were as gentle among you as a mother feeding and caring for her own children . . . ' (1 Thess. 2:7), and to the Corinthians, 'I am talking to you now as if you truly were my very own children . . . ' (2 Cor. 6:13).

There are many priests and ministers who, though single, nevertheless have real pastoral hearts, and they yearn and grieve over those given into their keeping, pray for them and rejoice with them, advise them and admonish them with true fatherly care. Because their 'availability' as fathers to the whole flock of God has developed their pastoral gifts to a greater degree than might otherwise have been possible, they are often quick to establish good relationships with children. The children in turn surround them with a sense of 'the family'.

One choice example of this was Father Dolling who worked for ten years in a Portsmouth slum. Although unorthodox in some of his methods and criticised, in his day, for some of his Tractarian sympathies, nevertheless he did an amazing work. Not only did he encourage a huge children's work with special Sunday Services and later day schools, he organised a number of clubs for boys, a boys' band and finally a club for gymnasts (having bought an old gymnasium).

From all parts of the world, strong, healthy self-respecting men, bless and praise God for the old gymnasium in Clarence Street. Some years ago, when I was at Vienna, I was watching a troupe of acrobats in one of the beer-gardens. They had reached their final feat by forming themselves into a living ladder, when suddenly, in a kind of ecstasy, I heard the topmost boy exclaim, 'Don't you see? there is the Father'; and before I knew where I was, three out of the five had precipitated themselves, and were clinging around me. There are scattered throughout the world today my brave army of gymnasium boys, but I believe they know that the Father's eye is still on them, and I know their love still compensates my heart for many of its sorrows.[1]

One of the deepest sorrows came when Fr. Dolling had to leave St. Agatha's, Portsmouth.

Even when I had to say, as I often had, hard, really hard things, with what love, what tenderness were they accepted. I, at any rate, shall never see the like again, for it is seldom granted twice to a man in his life to be called to a work like this, for they were all, in the truest sense, my own children; I had begotten them nearly all in Jesus Christ, and they have proved their loyalty not, I thank God, to me, but to our common Master.[2]

After he left St. Agatha's he received many letters from his former children in God. One of them began: 'Dear rev. farther, the new priest that come is so nice he do offer up some beautful prayers and speaks so nice to us all but ther will never be on that will be nearest our hearts as you dear farther . . .'[3]

[1] Fr. Dolling, *Ten Years in a Portsmouth Slum* (Brown and Longman), p. 30.
[2] Ibid., pp. 222-223.
[3] Ibid., p. 224.

Those single people who are in such professions as teaching, child care, youth leadership and children's nursing will inevitably, in the course of their work have opportunities of establishing close contacts with the young. With teachers and youth leaders, it is not only close but often a continuing and mutually enriching relationship. Pupils, for example, may think largely in terms of what the teachers have to give them, and be almost unaware of the ways in which they give to the teacher (other than when they give trouble!)

When I began teaching students, having previously taught in a girls' grammar school, I felt a great gap in my life and, at first, could not pinpoint the cause of this emptiness. Then it dawned on me that it was my younger charges at school whom I was missing. I missed their eager faces, their exuberance and their responsiveness. Particularly I missed the leg-pulls with which we used to start every lesson. Faced with rows of less *openly* responsive students, I did not at first feel free to tease them as mercilessly as I had my eleven to thirteen-year-olds (it came after a while!) for whose brightness and gaiety I ached. They had brought a particular joy that is a gift of childhood alone.

One school chaplain writing said:

Isn't it fun to live among the young? When school holidays come, it's lovely for ten days and then I long for the dear things to come back. I live on their vitality and am all of my 66 years when they aren't here . . . I play with the juniors (no, not lacrosse that terrifying pastime or blood-sport!) and we have all the VIth to tea in relays. How long I'll go on remains to be seen, but it is a thing of beauty and a joy, if not for ever. On the whole the girls teach me more than I teach them.

This, of course, highlights an important factor to remember. We may grow to love very deeply the children who have become our responsibility but we have to learn to love with a certain unattachedness. The people who perhaps have the hardest job are children's nurses or nannies. It is no easy thing to care for children as closely and devotedly as a nanny does and then to suffer a periodic termination of such 'motherhood' which must be no less than a form of death.

It is possible sometimes for single people to foster a child through the local authority but the same danger arises for them. Remembering the temporariness of the situation, it is essential not to become so emotionally attached to the child that the parting is a real 'tearing apart'. To bear in mind the eventual need to give back a child does not mean that the flow of love need be any the less, but both adult and child must know that separation is inevitable in the end.

Here I should like to pay tribute to a remarkable lady known to hundreds as 'Packie'. Together with a number of helpers she ran, for a good many years, a home for missionaries' children. Into that home she accepted tiny tots and babes in arms (whose parents were returning to pioneer missionary work where conditions were dangerous for small children) and brought them up for the absent parents, through toddlerhood, childhood and in some cases adolescence. She was their mother substitute; she was their security. Yet somehow the children were always conscious of the existence of their parents and of the fact that they 'belonged' to them. Packie kept the parents so constantly in the children's imagination and thoughts that they always existed for them as real people. And when eventually parents came home on furlough, the children were so well prepared for their arrival that most of them could run to them eagerly, not as strangers, but as 'Mummy' and 'Daddy'. Having nursed them through all their baby illnesses, heard their first words, watched their first faltering footsteps, taken them for their first day at school, noted their first efforts at reading and writing, she would then watch them leave her and go to the parents. Usually the parents took them away from the Home to a temporary furlough house. Sometimes it was for good. No matter what she felt or how deeply she loved a child, she had to relinquish her hold and give him back. Altogether this happened some eighty-four times! But although, at times, it would inevitably bring heartache, it did not bring heart*break* for she had learned to love without clinging.

Of course it was not the end of the relationship. Far from it! Her 'babes' still go back to her to share their successes and joys, their problems of broken marriages, childlessness, exam failures, unbelief; to ask advice; to sob out their hearts at their fears and frustrations; to speak shyly of their hopes. She still keeps in touch with most of them, cares about them, showers love on them, prays for them. But it is a love which, through the years, has been purged of all possessiveness. There are a host of her 'children' who thank God upon every remembrance of her. I should know. I am one of them!

There have been some cases where single people—or two single people—have been able to adopt children. Usually this happens only in very special circumstances. Adoption Societies do not make it easy for single people to adopt—and rightly so. There may, however, be unusual reasons that point to the wisdom of such a step. Where, however, there are long waiting lists of childless couples wanting to adopt babies, it is understandable that single people are discouraged. (With the widespread use of the pill and the activities consequent upon the Abortion Law, it seems that adoption will become even more difficult for single people in the future.) In this, as indeed in fostering, universal aunthood, or any other kind of child-minding, we need to be sure of our motives.

Whose needs are we primarily concerned about—our own or the child's? To 'use' a child as an outlet for our maternal or paternal instincts, as a means of alleviating our loneliness, of filling in the gaps in *our* lives, is to devalue him and treat him more as a pet.

So we return to the point from which we started this chapter. All single people need children in their lives, not as objects to be 'done good to' but as individuals with whom to have a loving, enriching relationship. We need them because they recall us to the path of simplicity where we regain our own lost childhood. This, after all, is the only path that leads to the Kingdom of God.

CHAPTER NINE

The Void

THIS BOOK IS A CONSIDERATION OF THE SINGLE LIFE, BUT IT would not deal adequately with the subject of those 'Who Walk Alone' if it said nothing of the position of those who, having known a real and loving partnership, suddenly find themselves alone. Death may suddenly leave them with a gaping hole in their lives. In their grief, it feels as though there has been a real mutilation of spirit as well as of family life. At first it is almost impossible to accept or adjust to the new situation. At such times as this, we need to know what the real needs of the bereaved are and to be clear as to how best we may help them.

Sometimes people are embarrassed at meeting bereaved people because they simply do not know what to say or do for the best, and their silence may almost appear as insensitivity. Yet it is far from mere nonchalance. It is simply uncertainty.

We need to remember first that the bereaved need to be ministered to in very loving ways. Because grief shatters some of our self-defence and leaves us almost stripped emotionally, a bereaved person may need actual physical comfort. There is that in us that still wants to run into our mother's arms for comfort when we are hurt, but as adults we cannot do that. Yet to be swept into a motherly or fatherly, sisterly or brotherly embrace and allowed to weep unashamedly and without causing embarrassment may sometimes bring tremendous comfort and release.

Sometimes the bereaved person is the kind of person who is more used to giving than receiving. Especially might this be so in the case of someone who has, for a long period, been nursing the person who has died, through a last illness. Through all that time, it has been necessary to think almost exclusively of the needs of the loved one, to prepare meals, comfort, cheer, read to, shop for and ease every burden of the dying person. There has only been time for giving. In bereavement, it is necessary to learn to receive. When there is a hole, let others fill it. 'The newly bereaved person needs periods of stabilising solitude both for physical rest and to gain perspective. In between, however, he needs to accept as fully as he can the love that flows from friends and family.'[1]

For some this is not altogether easy and there may well be a need to find ways in which the bereaved person can go on doing things for others as well as receiving as much as possible. Obviously after any death, there is a very difficult time of adjustment and the bereaved needs to be neither too fearful to receive help, love and support nor too overcome by self-pity to be able to pick up the pieces of life and go on. So, while the first need is for comfort and this will most certainly mean helping the bereaved to know the tremendous 'tenderness at the centre of heartbreak', it must be remembered that comfort has to do with strengthening and not just softness and sympathy. It may mean in some cases, firm encouragement, the taking of the hand, metaphorically, and setting a person on course again. For, one of the curious things that often penetrates the bewildered mind during bereavement is the fact that everybody else seems to be going about the daily routine in such a normal way, as though nothing had happened. Life does go on, and sooner or later one has to pick up the threads. Where a person is finding it really difficult to do this he needs the tenderness of sympathy and the firmness of love.

We need to be very careful, however, not to try and push someone into activity too soon. This is where it is so essential

[1] Catherine Marshall, *To Live Again* (Hodder and Stoughton), p. 51.

to be sensitive to the real needs of the bereaved. Sometimes well-intentioned people assume that if there is a gap, which undoubtedly there is, it must be filled with activity—'to take their minds off it' they say! There is a great danger here of forcing the pace and preventing the healing processes from taking their proper time and course. The healing may take a very long time, but there is an initial stage of numbness and shock in which it is unwise to press a person into activity. They may accept some kind of work very readily but if it comes too soon on top of the shock, it may in fact be a form of flight from the reality of the situation. To live life, as Catherine Marshall puts it, 'on the busy—busy level, dragging an anaesthetised spirit after one', may provide a temporary refuge from the awful truth but it is not the real answer. It requires a day to day acceptance of the situation and an honest facing of the fact of death so that, little by little, it is accepted positively. We may be able to run away from some things fairly success- fully, but grief is the one thing from which we cannot run away, It always catches up with us sooner or later.

There are, of course, certain things that have to be done— and done immediately. The 'mechanics of death' such as registering the death, arranging the funeral service, contacting relatives, etc., may, in a strange way, be quite a comfort. In any case, there are still meals to get and washing to be done and all the household chores to be considered. There is a certain therapy for a broken heart in having some practical things to do especially in the first few days of numbness. Simon Peter needed his practical tasks after the death of Jesus and said 'I'm going fishing'. The others said, 'We'll come too'. So while it would be wrong to press someone into activity too soon, it would also be unwise to insist on doing everything for them. They need the comfort of some of the practical everyday jobs that do not carry any heavy responsibility with them.

The real shock is likely to take hold of a bereaved person a week or ten days after the death, or even longer in the case of delayed shock. So it is as well to remember that, as far as possible in that period of shock, no major decisions should be taken, and no irrevocable changes made.

Sometimes it is felt that a swift change of setting is the best way to hasten the healing processes for the heartbroken, to sell up the home that holds so many memories, and move to a new area and a completely new life. There may be no choice in the matter. It is one of the sad things about clergy widows that, in losing their husbands, they often lose their homes too—unless they are amongst the fortunate few who have been able to buy their own homes. The same is true of course, of others whose houses 'go with the job'. Widowers are not usually placed in that harrowing position, but widows, in these circumstances, may need a lot of practical help and a great deal of supportive friendship. Generally speaking, however, a change of setting is not necessarily a good thing. It may be the right course for some, but for many it would be quite wrong. At a time of loss, it may well be a very great comfort to be amongst one's friends and neighbours, in a familiar environment. To be surrounded by the once shared possessions, to see the well loved, familiar pictures, books and garden may be balm to a hurt soul, rather than pain and, besides having a soothing effect, the 'familiar things' help to give a sense of continuity to life.

One of the deepest needs at a time of bereavement is to be able to *externalise* grief. Full healing cannot come until it has been thus externalised. We need to let our emotions surface so it is quite wrong (and probably harmful) to try and hide them at such a time. It is all the more important therefore to be surrounded by those whom we know and love well, our 'comfortable' friends with whom we can weep or let rip in an angry outburst, or on to whom we can even offload some of our self-pity and self-reproach, our fears and our worries. It does not need the counsellor's training to be able to stand alongside a person in his/her grief, but it *does* need someone who is sufficiently relaxed, understanding and secure to be able to let the bereaved person simply talk or cry it out. The wise friend will not try to stem the flow of words or tears but will wait quietly until the emotional wells have dried up for the time being.

WHERE ARE THEY NOW?

One question which is bound to clamour (inwardly if not outwardly) for an answer, is this: 'Where is my loved one now? Does he still exist?' Clearly the bodily form, as they have known it, is dead and must be disposed of by burial or burning. But *is* that the end? Some will answer quite categorically 'Yes'. *In one sense* the adjustment for them may be easier. Their loved one no longer 'exists' any more than a house that has been demolished 'exists'. Certainly many atheists would claim to think in that way, but even atheists can become agnostic in the face of death. Others are certain that there *is* a life beyond death but want to know what sort of life it is. If their belief is not informed by their religious faith, they may try to 'pick the lock' of that unknown realm and, through the help of clairvoyants and spiritualists, seek to make contact with their loved one. This can be a dangerous way of dealing with our doubts.

For those of us who stand by someone at a time of loss, one should remember that even for those of deep, orthodox Christian faith, there may be agonising questions which, sadly, they feel less able to articulate because they fear it might seem like a denial of all that they have believed. Surely it is right to bring those questions and doubts out into the open. If you have them, you cannot get rid of them by pretending they don't exist. So often our beliefs about life after death are accepted cerebrally, and it is not until we are faced with the actual situation of death that we have to work through our questions at a deeper emotional and spiritual level. Intellectual acceptance then becomes a small part of the total acceptance of a belief in the life beyond and, it is from the depths of one's being as well as the top of one's mind that one cries out, 'Lord, I believe. Help thou my unbelief.'

More often than not, for the believer of longstanding Christian faith, the questions are somewhat different. He or she may not ask so much 'Where is my loved one? Does he still exist?' as 'What is my relationship to him now?' As Catherine Marshall said:

> That brought me to a question my every emotion cried out to have answered. What is my relationship to my husband now? In marriage I had found my identity, my answer to the question, 'Who am I?' As a woman, much of my orientation in life had been centred in my relationship to one man. It is this way with most women. Then when death cleaves the marriage partnership, the woman left alone feels that her whole basis for living has been washed out. She must begin all over again . . . 'Who am I now?'[1]

Love of course continues, but is it still the two-way love that we have known? How can that love be expressed since clearly it cannot have physical forms of expression? One longs to cry out and share things with the partner one knew so well. Is it wrong to go on talking to them as though they were still here, with physical ears with which to listen? Can they, in fact, hear us in their new existence?

There are so many ways of communicating even in this life and human speech is only one of these many ways. It seems reasonable to suppose (for those of us who believe in a life beyond) that thought life continues. So just as thoughts can be communicated and transferred without words to those on the wave length of love here, so surely there is much traffic in our thought life with those beyond. Is this not *part* of the meaning of the Communion of Saints? Certainly that communion means our togetherness in the body of Christ. Certainly it involves our joint activity, worshipping God either here on earth or in His nearer presence. But I feel sure that flowing through that

---

[1] op. cit., p. 27.

channel of love that cannot be broken, is a wealth of understanding, healing, insight, inspiration, compassion, encouragement, good sense and humour too.

In the midst of writing this book, my ex-Principal who had
been giving me such a lot of help and advice, and to whom I
have dedicated this book, died. Initially I felt very bereft but
then faith soared and I refused to believe that she was unable
to go on encouraging and prompting simply because cancer had
robbed us of her physical presence. So often we tend to imagine
the life beyond in spatial terms and there seems to be a vast
distance fixed between us and those who have died, whereas it
may be much nearer the truth to think of that other world as
interpenetrating this one and a good deal closer to us than we
have ever conceived. The veil between the seen and the
unseen is often very thin.

Some may feel what I say now is no more than pious claptrap, but I believe prayer, for the believer, is tremendously
important, particularly at a time of bereavement. It can be
dismissed as merely a temporary source of comfort. Some may
feel it is dishonest to turn to prayer when in a crisis, but many
of us believe that Richard Baxter put his finger right on the
truth when he spoke of meeting with our loved ones before the
throne of God as joint petitioners. Where may I meet my loved
one? The answer surely is in prayer and worship, for daily we
can meet together in that activity which most draws us together
anyway.

> In the blest fellowship of saints
> Is wisdom safety and delight;
> And when my heart declines and faints,
> It's raised by their heat and light.
>
> As for my friends, they are not lost;
> The several vessels of thy fleet,
> Though parted now, by tempests tost,
> Shall safely in the haven meet.

Still we are centred all in thee,
Members, though distant, of one Head;
In the same family we be,
By the same faith and Spirit led.

Before thy throne we daily meet
As joint-petitioners to thee,
In spirit we each other greet,
And shall again each other see.[1]

That is the sure and certain hope that enables believers to
bring a real note of triumph and joy into the midst of their
sorrowing. It has often been the rejoicing faith of Christians
at funerals that has confounded those of other faiths, as many
Christian missionaries will testify.

THE PRACTICAL PROBLEMS

There are of course practical problems to be faced by those
who suddenly find themselves walking alone. For a widow it
may mean finding a job again, or, in the case of someone who
married very young, for the first time. The whole pattern and
routine of life have to be changed. It presents great difficulties
if she has no previous training or qualifications and may
involve undertaking some training or a refresher course while
still coping with a family. Much will depend upon the provision
made by the husband, in the way of insurances, as to how
quickly she needs to get work. For some it has to be almost at
once. This is where again, it is wise for a widow to remain
amongst those friends and neighbours she has known who can
perhaps help at times by looking after the children or offering
transport, generally supporting her and giving advice as she
re-adjusts.

Another area in which she may need help is simply in the
matter of coping with the paper work. One widow said that

[1] Richard Baxter, 'He wants not friends that hath Thy love.'

never before had she had so many forms to fill in and so many pamphlets to read. At first it can be very bewildering and some widows are singularly ill-equipped to meet this side of life — as this confession reveals:

In many ways, I was still a little girl. I had adored and leaned on my husband. Like many a sheltered woman who had married young, I had never once figured out our income-tax form, had a car inspected, consulted a lawyer, or tried to read an insurance policy. Rail-road timetables and plane schedules were enigmas to me. My household accounts rarely balance. I had never invested money. I had been driving a car for only three months . . . now I was faced with all these practical problems and many, many more.

There was some insurance but not enough . . . I was not trained to earn a living. I had married when my college diploma was warm from the dean's hand, before I had even earned a teacher's certificate . . . The adjustment that faced me, therefore, posed a challenge in every way in which a woman can be challenged.[1]

One of the kindest gestures that perhaps one can offer a widow is some help and advice on these practical matters. She may be too proud to ask for help because she feels her incompetence is pitiable, and friends may hesitate to offer help especially if it demands a degree of trust and personal knowledge of financial affairs. Nevertheless it could be an offer that would be seized with enormous relief and might possibly reduce anxiety more than anything else.

The bereaved person will have to face loneliness. However much your friends help, they can never fill the place of the one you loved. But friends who are sensitive to this inevitable pain can alleviate it greatly by seeing that the bereaved person is not completely cut off from all social life. Widowers tend to

[1] Catherine Marshall, *To Live Again*, pp. 22-23.

fare rather better here. People often express their concern in practical ways like cooking for them. Because men are supposed to be slightly more helpless about cooking than women, people often feel and express a mothering concern. They are invited out to meals and quite often stay on after the meal to share the evening with their friends. Since it is assumed that women are able to cook for themselves, there is not always this form of immediate practical concern. For a widow it can be lonely if she has no family, and yet equally lonely if she has, that is, a young family which necessitates staying in in the evenings. While they are too young to be left, she may feel a real sense of isolation. Not only will she probably welcome visitors. She will probably appreciate offers of baby-sitters so that she can get out even though on her own. In a letter, one widow complained that, since her husband's death, their friends had stopped inviting her out. She was particularly hurt by one couple whom she and her husband had visited almost weekly for bridge until his death and who, since that, had not invited her to their home at all. It would be very hard indeed if a widow found that she was not wanted by anyone for herself alone but discovered that she had only ever been looked upon as an adjunct to her husband. It would surely be a rare situation where that occurred. But perhaps it points out a need for the married woman to have her own friends as well as those friends which she shares with her husband. And it also highlights the need to keep an open door for widows and those lonely and in distress at a time when all looks rosy. One wonders how often the newly bereaved widow, who complained that she never received any invitations out, had herself opened her home to widows, spinsters and lonely folk when her husband was alive?

Sometimes people can only face up to loneliness in solitude. All the invitations out cannot heal the hurt, and may in fact only provoke further strain because it means putting a brave face on things. Here we need great wisdom to be able to distinguish between those times when it would be right to encourage a person to be gregarious, and those times when it is right to respect their longing for solitude. Whatever we do to try and fill up their days, the loneliness must still be faced. By forcing people to flee from it during the day-time, we may only be ensuring that they will have it in concentrated form at night, when wave upon wave of it will flood over them. No one can stand by and help then.

The nights are often the hardest anyway. Suddenly the lack of companionship hits home and the longing for physical tenderness is almost unbearable, the strong arm to wrap around in comfort, the shoulder to cry on, the listening ear. As time goes on, there is the sex hunger to be faced. Those for whom sexual activity has had a meaningful and satisfying place in their marital lives are obviously going to have problems when such activity has to stop abruptly. The strong-minded man who says: 'From this point on, I am going to give up smoking!' and does, is not necessarily going to be immune from all cravings for a cigarette. The man who is told by his doctor that he must never play football again, will still have to live with his longings. All of us have sexual appetites, but those who are single have usually begun to channel that appetite and its energies into other ways. The newly bereaved person has not usually learned to do that because it has not been necessary. His energies have found their proper outlet in marital sex. Here then is another big adjustment to be made, one which may be harder for the widower than the widow.

What is the answer? Some rediscover the habit of masturbation and suffer the renewal of teenage guilt. Others claim that they can practise this without guilt, in which case it might be a right, if temporary answer, for here masturbation is not so much linked with mental activity as with a physical need. Nerves and muscles have been accustomed to certain forms of excitement and soothing and the *sudden* cessation of this is too difficult.

The long-term answer for those who find it difficult to adjust to the 'walk alone' may be re-marriage, and the proportion of widowers who re-marry is high. Far from disloyalty, it could really be seen as a compliment to the first wife, for it is usually those who have been deeply happy in marriage who find that the walk alone is intolerable. Those who have been unhappily married may well be more wary of entering into matrimony for a second time.

THE DIVORCEE

This is not always the case as we must recognise as we come to look at that other group who are sometimes plunged very sadly and, maybe, suddenly into the lonely walk—the divorcees. Much of what has been said about bereavement would be applicable to those whose partnership ends through divorce, except that if the marriage has been unhappy for a long time, the ending of it may bring considerable relief. The awful strain of tension and cold war will probably have token its toll and the divorcee has reached the end of his or her endurance anyway.

It is impossible to say if, for example, a woman suffers more by maintaining an almost intolerable partnership than by having it dissolved; at the time of dissolution she is probably quite sure it is intolerable. After the dissolution she may not be quite sure. Either way there is bound to be heartache and suffering. A woman needs to be particularly sure that she is doing the right thing by seeking a divorce, because she is the main loser if a marriage ceases.

The ordinary loneliness which takes the place of a man about the house is particularly painful to a woman because she has probably, for many years, planned her life around looking after that man. All the polishing and redecorating, dusting and scrubbing have been not just for herself, but for his comfort. The food has probably largely been chosen to suit his taste, perhaps to conform to his diet; when he goes it is possible that the garden will go to weeds and the car be sold because these were his part of the household. His parents

who called so regularly may have been old friends—what do
they now become? And his friends who were hers too—are
they totally lost?

Quite often of course, the home itself has to be sold when
the family possessions are divided, but even in new surround-
ings there is an emptiness to the day, unbroken by a husband
coming home from work, or having to be roused in the
mornings.[1]

Apart from material loss and upheaval, there is the wretched
ordeal of the divorce proceedings and, once these are over, the
terrible sense of humiliation. Nearly everyone goes out in
sympathy to the widow, but there is more reserve in the case of
the ex-wife. 'There are always two sides to a broken marriage'
people are quick to observe. Often they are more embarrassed
at mentioning an ex-husband or wife than a late one. Divorcee
wives, as with widows, claim that when the husband goes they
are sometimes ostracised by friends they have known for years.
They are not invited to parties because they would make an odd
number (why do parties have to be run on neat, mathematical
lines?) Sometimes they feel they are excluded because there is a
kind of stigma about them, or the hostesses fear that they will be
entertaining man-hunters.

To be reasonable, there is a period of time after or immediately before divorce when a man or woman (particularly a
woman) would not want to enter into social activities very
much. They are not ready to meet the gaze of their friends.
Wounds may still be open, especially if they are in a state of
separation before divorce. When, for example, a woman has
been deserted by her husband quite unexpectedly (and we all
know cases where husbands have just walked out on their
wives), she will need a long time to re-adjust, to sort out her
confused feelings, to decide about the future, and to come to
terms with her wounded pride. It would be quite unfeeling to
expect her to 'snap out of it' and try to involve her in a round

[1] Evelyn Home, *Personal Problems Today.*

of gay social events. To be truly sensitive to such people, you must not only try and understand their pain and humiliation and give the right kind of sympathy but you must also try and assess their financial position. They may say they prefer to remain at home on their own simply because they cannot afford outings. With much tact it might be possible to get them to join a party if they know they are going *as a guest*.

All of us will, at some stage, know the pain of bereavement and some will have known it already. Not all of us will experience the pain of divorce. It is all the more important therefore that we should try to enter imaginatively into this particular kind of suffering so that we can be truly helpful to those in distress, giving a non-judgmental and practical compassion.

Two further observations may be made here. The first concerns the need for *continuing* care. At the time of a death, people are full of sympathy for the bereaved family. They write letters, send cards and flowers and remember them in prayer and send out waves of love and compassion. It is at such times that one really discovers how wonderful friends and neighbours can be. One is buoyed up and carried along by their love and sympathy. There is a real sense of being sustained. But what of six months later? or even a year later? Often it is then, when the initial shock and numbness have completely passed, that the reaction sets in. There needs to be as much, possibly more, loving support then. Yet we so quickly grow used to the idea that someone has died, and we settle back into our old ways, adjusting to this as a fact. We may not continue to be so actively concerned or mindful of the needs of the bereaved one who may have adjusted on the surface, but inwardly is still far from being healed.

The second observation concerns those who actually suffer bereavement. At the time of death, when everyone is being so loving and sympathetic, there is no need to make immediate and huge efforts to get up and go on. No one expects a bereaved person to impose upon himself heavier strains than he is already bearing but, if after several weeks and months, he is not making any effort to come back into normality, then sympathy may well begin to wear thin and there may be a marked cooling off in interest. On the other hand everyone applauds the courage of the person, who after the initial shock, begins to plan and adjust for the future and makes a brave come-back. They will continue to back him or her up and offer help, encourage him and include him in their plans.

So while for the one group it is necessary to remember that sympathy must not cease as soon as the funeral is over but needs continuing, overt expression, for the other it is necessary to remember that some effort to help oneself will bring a most encouraging, sympathetic response from friends.

One practical step that may be helpful to a bereaved person is to take up some form of social work. The grief that comes with a death often leaves us mellower and more tender hearted. Sometimes we marvel that a person is so compassionate, and then discover that it is suffering that has made them so. Maybe the experience of this form of suffering makes a person eminently suitable for some form of service, so that far from being a negative experience, bereavement can equip a person with a positive gift to offer.

RETIREMENT

The other void we should consider here is caused through retirement. Here men may be the greater suffers. Women have such a strong home-making instinct that, even if a woman has to retire at sixty or sixty-five, she is never really without a job or lost as to how to spend her leisure time. Some in fact are so busy in retirement that they wonder how they ever fitted in a job as well. Men, however, may find themselves with time on their hands at first, but most remedy this pretty quickly. The void for them is not really one of minutes and hours so much as status.

12

At sixty-five a man has usually gained a fair amount of respect in his place of work, he probably holds a position of responsibility. Men often identify with their jobs; even those who have grumbled consistently about their work find a good deal of satisfaction in their status and the respect which it brings them. At retirement, the loss of the job seems to them to mean loss of status and therefore loss of importance. No wonder some men feel in quite a panic just before retirement, even if outwardly they appear to be looking forward to their so called 'freedom'. Who will look up to him now? Who will recognise his worth and ability?

Many men get part-time jobs so that the initial panic does not last long, but it is a good idea to have a plan of action for the first week or two of retirement. If possible a holiday should be arranged but otherwise outings and day trips and visits to friends and relations will relieve the feeling of emptiness and do away with the aimlessness that leads to boredom.

Some psychologists say that, ideally, everyone, be they male or female, should begin to plan for retirement at the time that they map out their main career. This seems an exaggeration. It is scarcely likely that the Careers Master at school is going to advise a teenager on retirement. But it *is* realistic to suggest that in the forties and fifties people should plan for retirement. The Pre-Retirement Association will help here (26, Bedford Square, London, W.C.1.) and some local Education Authorities run courses on preparing for retirement.

We are all aware of the need to plan financially — indeed that part of the preparation is often undertaken for us by compulsory superannuation schemes — but there is much more to planning retirement than the financial aspect. We need to know the value of time and how best to use it — a lesson that concerns much of our life. As children we had little sense of time. We dawdled and loitered, all of us at times driving adults to distraction. The years, however, have taught us punctuality and how to work to a time schedule, but in the pressure of a busy working life, we may have failed to learn the vital art of how to make time for those leisure activities that relax us and re-create us. If we have never made time to develop hobbies and interests that really fulfil us and that we enjoy and love to share with others, then retirement is going to bring problems. Not only will time hang heavily, but if we have lived in a world of total work and our friends have all been associated with our job, we are going to miss their companionship terribly. And we will not have had time or opportunity to cultivate any other friendships so that, added to boredom, there may be loneliness. It is all very well to think in terms of taking up this and that, and joining the local golf club or bird-watching society or car club. But it may be that, in spite of pension schemes, we have to learn to live on a much lower income than we did, and there may not be much left for the luxury of joining different societies.

It is good to develop in the middle years hobbies and interests that can then be continued at retirement. There is no reason why anyone should stagnate. If the hobbies can be well balanced—some involving mental activity and others of a more practical nature—it will bring us in contact with different groups of people and widen our circle of friends. A person who has learned to read for his own enjoyment, who keeps in touch with many people through a network of letters, who has cultivated the art of conversation and therefore makes a very welcome and acceptable visitor, can really look forward to retirement as a time when these things will not have to compete with a host of other activities for a place in his personal agenda. There will now be far more time for them and he will be a much sought-after person.

Not only must the question of 'What to do?' be faced in retirement, but also that of 'Where to go?' Sometimes it is imperative to move. The reduced income leaves no choice. Those who have been forced to live in cities may hanker after a bit of country life. The thing to be remembered in reaching a decision about this is that in retirement we *need* a community to which we can belong. If it is possible to move into a village where there is a strong sense of community and there is no question but that we shall be welcome, then it sounds ideal. If, however, we are attracted by a cottage miles out in a lonely part of the country far away from the nearest village and shops, then we should consider carefully before rushing into it. How easy will it be to get to know people? We shall need friends in an isolated place like that for what happens if we are ill, or snowed in, or frozen out?

There is much to be said for retiring within the community where we have lived and worked, where people know us, love us, and accept us for ourselves. If we have received richly *from* the community in the past, then it gives us an opportunity to put something back into it. If we are members of a church, it may give us the chance to take on some of the jobs we have never had time to do before. We may be able to enjoy our friends and neighbours in a way that was quite impossible during the years we were commuting to work.

To move or not to move? That can be *the* question. There are advantages on both sides and the decision may rest largely with our temperament and bank balance. If we bear in mind however that wherever we live, we shall need to be part of a community, we shall be wise to have the stimuli of libraries, clubs, theatres, etc., that we shall need opportunities of service either in a church or political party or with voluntary social organisations, that we shall need to find a home within our income bracket that will be of manageable size as we get older and the garden of which we shall be able to cope with fairly easily, it should help us to make the right choice.

One other way in which we can prepare for retirement is by cultivating a love of solitude. This cannot be done overnight and must be started much earlier in life. There are some who live their lives in a whirl of frenzied activism and keep this up till the last of the retirement dinners is over. Retirement for them must be hard and perhaps only possible at first with the aid of tranquillisers. However, to have developed a love of outward solitude that leads to inner solitude which in turn frees us from the distraction of ourselves and other people for God is a most valuable lesson. We can begin to practise this at an early age, and the younger the better, by disciplining ourselves. When we find ourselves alone for an evening, what do we do?

Rush around to our nearest friend to spend the evening together with *someone*?

Get on to the phone for long conversations?

Busy ourselves with non-essential household chores?

But why not stay alone and simply be still?

Maybe listen to a little music?

Do some quiet reflecting on life?

Remember friends we have scarcely had time to think of in the weeks of busyness?

Enjoy having the cat on our lap, or the dog on the mat in front of us?

Look at (not just glance at) the paintings on the wall that we by-pass every day in our hurry and see in them again the qualities that attracted us in the first place?

If we have built up a cosy little home, then why not just sit in it (quite still) and enjoy it? Have you ever had a lengthy period of illness when you have lain in one room? By the end of the illness you know every detail of the room and the shape of the trees out of the window and the different parts of the pictures on the wall that are highlighted by the sun at different times of the day. Lying there, you may have reached some pretty clear thoughts about life, its meaning, its purpose and *your* place in the scheme of things. Eventually you emerge from bed, weaker and thinner maybe, but with a clearer perspective and a sense that this suffering had been creative. But why do we need to wait until we are ill to experience this quality of life? Solitude is something for which we should make time regularly, learning to enjoy it and the heightened awareness that comes with it. Through it too, we can learn to enjoy the companionship of

God whose resources are as adequate to meet the needs of our retirement as they have been during our working lives.

The time comes to most of us when whether we like it or not, old age and failing powers force us into solitude. Many people dread this time, and of course we can't relapse into laziness and become increasingly a burden to others—we must keep going while we can. But inevitably we shall become more and more alone. If we have longed for solitude, and learned to love it because we find God there, it should be that the last years of a long life will be the happiest of all, lived so close to Him that His life and love can shine through us to bless countless souls.[1]

[1] Sister Phoebe, C.S.M.V., unpublished letter to Oblates.

CHAPTER TEN

Practical Consideration of Singleness

1. HOME-MAKING

MUCH OF WHAT I HAVE SAID SO FAR HAS DEALT WITH the emotional aspects of 'walking alone'. Let us look in some detail at practical aspects of the problem, the disadvantages and the advantages. We shall not concern ourselves with such minor things as the car that won't start, or how best to break into your house if you shut yourself out, though these are annoying things that happen to us all. For the most part we have neighbours on whom we can call if we are stuck in such emergencies, and many of us who are single would gratefully acknowledge the wonderful neighbours we have had.

What I want to look at in this chapter are those things which cannot be undertaken by neighbours. They are the situations in which even our friends may not be able to help.

A PLACE OF ONE'S OWN

Home-making is an instinct in all of us, married or single. We each need our nest, with or without a mate. What is more and quite contrary to some older beliefs, home-making is important for men as well as women! A bachelor needs his 'pad', a place of his own where he can put down roots and entertain his friends, enjoy his hobbies and escape the pressures of work. The Englishman's castle is his home—whether he shares it with a wife and family or not.

Nowadays, with so many household gadgets to reduce housework to the minimum, a single man can look after himself very well indeed. We should remember that, for every single man whose flat is a mess, who never cooks a proper meal and who has an overflowing laundry basket, there are an equal number of single women in the same boat. It is not that they do not want to be efficient. It is just that there are so many demands on their time that the running of the home cannot be a priority.

If then, the need to be a home-maker is there in each of us, it is important to cater for that need. Some people have the wonderful knack of turning any kind of a dwelling into 'home'.

Corrie Ten Boom (in *The Hiding Place*) tells the story of how she and her sister Betsie were imprisoned in a concentration camp and put into separate cells. Corrie was in isolation in one cell whereas Betsie was in a cell with a number of other women. One day Corrie was tipped off that, if she walked slowly down a certain corridor, she would see her sister. It was only a fleeting glimpse—the door of Betsie's cell was open and she was just able to see inside for a two or three second flash. Betsie, with her flair for turning any room into a lovely home, had even managed to transform a crowded prison cell into a place of taste and beauty. Corrie could scarcely believe what she saw. She wrote:[1]

For unbelievably, against all logic, this cell was charming. My eyes seized only a few details as I inched reluctantly past. The straw pallets were rolled instead of piled in a heap, standing like pillars along the walls, each with a lady's hat atop it. A headscarf had somehow been hung along the wall. The contents of several food packages were arranged on a

[1] Corrie Ten Boom, *The Hiding Place* (Hodder and Stoughton).

small shelf; I could just hear Betsie saying, 'The red biscuit tin here in the centre!' Even the coats hanging on their hooks were part of the welcome of that room, each sleeve draped over the shoulder of the coat next to it like a row of dancing children.

The stamp of her own lovely personality was upon it, as it had been upon their home in Scheveningen.

What are the prerequisites of good home-making? First and obviously, you must *have* a home. In the case of Betsie Ten Boom, it was officially her father's house, but, with her mother dead, she was mistress of the house. Freedom is an important factor here, freedom to cultivate tastes and express oneself artistically in the home. Most people need to get away from their parents' home just because of this need for real freedom.

What should single people do about acquiring a home? What are the alternatives for those who have left their parental home and have perhaps moved into a completely different area?

INTO DIGS

You can, of course, go into digs, and many young men leaving home for the first time do this, especially if they are not sure how long they will be staying in that area. Digs may well be a good first step — though much will depend on the landlady. Some landladies are wonderful, cooking excellent meals and looking after the washing and ironing in a capable and motherly way. Digs then become a real home from home, and mothers are relieved that their sons, and in some cases daughters, are being properly looked after. Other landladies can so hem a lodger in with rules and regulations, with nagging and fussing, that he is loth to go back to his digs. He would prefer to roam the streets or sit it out in the cinema rather than face such a restricting atmosphere. It is when young people start a job in a big city away from all their friends and find themselves in none too satisfactory digs that they may take to wandering the streets, looking for company in clubs and groups rather than face the appalling loneliness big cities can bring. The company may not always be desirable but anything is better than being alone or spending an evening with a grousing landlady.

It is for such young people that churches could, should and often do, provide a refuge—a place to go and a centre of friendship.

It is important, therefore, to look for good digs, so if the first choice turns out to be a bad one—then change. There is no obligation to stick it out and make life a misery. It may be necessary to pay a week or more's board in advance but it is better to forfeit that than continue in an unhappy situation. So shop around until you find digs that *really* suit you, where you can relax and feel at home, where it is not essential to escape out on to the streets after the meal each evening.

Ideally, however, digs should be regarded as just a stepping stone to greater independence. Some people go on living in digs for years on end and seem quite content to continue in that kind of dependence. They are apparently happy to accept the routine, customs, tastes and habits of someone else's family home. Usually they are not free to switch their meal times, or decorate their room with some way-out wallpaper, or have the run of the house at their own convenience for a party. It may be very nice to have your meals cooked and set before you—with no preparation and perhaps no washing-up. It is lovely to find your shirts neatly washed and ironed and socks carefully darned, and your room cleaned and dusted regularly, but that is not real freedom. You cannot just live your life without any reference to the host family. You are not free to accept an on-the-spot invitation to a meal out, if you know one is being prepared for you. You cannot always wear just what you choose if you are governed by the housewife's routine in washing and ironing. You cannot stay away for a night or bring a friend home for a meal, without letting your landlady know.

Maybe these are small considerations when weighed against the excellent service given but young people should be careful not to sell themselves into a bondage of this kind. Often they hope to get away from some of the restrictions of living at home, but find that the restrictions of a landlady are even tighter! Rarely will she put up with the treatment and inconsideration that some mothers get! To continue in this way is surely substituting one mother figure for another, and does not seem to be promoting independence or aiding the growing-up process.

Having taken the first, possibly hesitant, step forward and broken away from home by going into digs, a young bachelor or single girl may then decide to plunge into the greater freedom of renting a flat or bedsitter. Here at least they can look after themselves and cook their meals. Even though they are only renting and the property is not their own to decorate or alter as they will, at least they can be self-contained. Actually a number of landlords or landladies are willing for tenants to do a certain amount of decorating. If not, however, there are always a few pieces of your own furniture that can be painted or re-upholstered. It may be necessary to use the furniture already in the flat or 'bed-sit', but it is usually possible to decide upon a predominant colour and see that your own ornaments, curtains, tablecloths, mats, etc., fit into the colour scheme. Here at least, one can begin to play with ideas and develop a sense of taste where colours and the arrangement of personal possessions are concerned. There is also freedom to entertain and experiment with all sorts of concoctions in the kitchen.

RENTING

Renting in this way is ideal if, for various reasons, it is not possible to put down any more permanent roots. If a person is uncertain as to how long he is going to stay in one place, temporary accommodation is obviously the right thing. More often than not, it is the financial position that is the deciding factor. Young people were rarely able to save enough in the initial years of work to put down a deposit on a house in order to buy it, and now find it impossible with such high rates of interest. Nor is it always the younger generation who find themselves thus handicapped. Renting then is the only way open to them.

As soon as it *is* possible to start buying a flat or house, young people should seriously consider such a step. For whatever you pay in rent (and it may be a great deal per week) you never have any return on that money. It is so easy to get into a vicious circle from which it seems almost impossible to break out. If, for example, one is paying £12 per week in rent on a flat (and this is a low figure now especially in London and other cities), it will probably mean that that together with living expenses make it impossible to put aside any savings. If you cannot save, then you cannot begin to think of buying.

BUYING

I am convinced that 'a place of one's own' should be the goal of every single person, male and female. It may take a long time to reach that point, but I am sure that to own a place of your own is a major step forward in life and independence. I say *place* because it may not actually be a house or flat. Some friends of mine who could not afford a house bought a houseboat and, by skilful interior decoration, turned it into a delightfully cosy and attractive home. Two children were born to them during their time on the boat, and they also had a very large dog, but there was no sense of crush. Houseboats can, of course, be exceedingly expensive living quarters—it depends upon the area. Caravans are often far cheaper propositions—or perhaps one should give them the more euphemistic term, 'mobile homes'. Somehow caravans are still associated with gypsy life and often people do not realise what very comfortable, roomy and economic homes they can be. If they are on proper sites with main drainage and electricity, there is very little apparent difference between caravan life and that in a bungalow or flat. They offer one way of living sufficiently cheaply to be able to save for a house, for once the caravan is bought the only other expenses are site rents, electricity and Calor gas, and possibly rates if it is not a Corporation site. Like cars, a caravan will warm up very quickly but it does not retain the heat in the same way that a house will. Nevertheless they are very economical to heat and light. They tend to rock in the wind but are usually so well insulated that draughts are rarely a problem. You are also insulated from the noise of neighbours far more effectively than in many flats. It is essential of course, to ensure that a caravan home is placed on a well-organised site with the required minimum space between each caravan, adequate facilities and protection from fire and noise.

Like cars, caravans depreciate in value rapidly but while the selling price may be low, at least while you live in a caravan the 'overheads' do not amount to much. Almost all the repair jobs can be done without calling in specialist help and decorating is very easy and straightforward.

It is worth considering then these rather modest movements towards complete independence. Even in a houseboat or caravan, you have a chance to taste the full joys of *having* a home. At least it *is* your own and psychologically that is highly desirable. Many single people would testify that, once they got a home of their own, they felt 'settled'. A gap in their lives had been filled. However small the place may be, it *is* home and the place where you can either shut the door on the world and seek solitude, or you can open it wide to the world and invite people to come and share the warmth, the love, the fun, the peace of *your* home. What you create in a home is an atmosphere — not a show place, and it is that that draws people. Here is a home stamped with the personality of the owner. Here a welcome, friendship, sympathy and deep interest are guaranteed. Here you can be more fully yourself. That is what anyone can do with a home, single people included. And it can be done on a shoestring!

One of the warmest, most open and friendly homes I know is that of a couple who have recently been bankrupt. There is a great wealth in that home, even though they are living under a terrible financial strain. The door is almost always open and friends come and go in a steady stream. An incredible variety of people descend on this one humble couple from all parts of the world and no one is ever turned away. Coffee is always brewing, conversation is always flowing. No matter who you are, or what your language, you are all drawn into the circle of friendship. The small living-room seems literally to expand as more and more visitors flow in. This couple who have so little in terms of worldly possessions, have taught me much about home-making. It is this great openness and sharing of *themselves* with all who come to them that constitutes the foremost ingredient of their home. Their's is a place where people find love and, often, the solution to deep personal problems. There are no special counselling techniques, yet a good number have found healing simply through the complete acceptance they have found here.

I maintain that the goal of everyone should be a home of one's own and ultimately that home should be in bricks and mortar. For while a caravan or boat depreciates in value fairly rapidly, a house appreciates equally rapidly. The price of houses has risen very steeply over recent years and the buying of property if you can do it, is a very sound financial investment. The taking on of a mortgage is a form of compulsory saving—but immensely worthwhile.

If a single person feels that he/she is reaching the point where it may be possible really to 'launch out into the deep' and take that further, most important, step towards freedom, then he/she should arrange to see his/her bank manager and put him fully in the picture.

Perhaps I should explode a myth here. There are single people, particularly women, who imagine it is impossible to get a mortgage loan if single. This is certainly not true—there are many single women and bachelors who are buying their own homes. It is true, however, that there are often greater difficulties for the single house buyer (and these have increased with the sharp rise in mortgage rates). Generally a proportion only of the wife's salary is taken into consideration when applications for a mortgage are made, nevertheless a double salary obviously does make it easier for a married couple than for a single person who has the mortgage repayment, rates and other outgoing expenses on the house as well as living costs to come out of one monthly cheque.

Each of the 450 building societies in this country has its own yardstick for granting a loan. Some base the amount of the loan on income only. Some take outgoings, number of children and repairs into consideration as well; others include part of the wife's earnings. Many will not lend to self-employed persons or someone with an unstable occupation. Single women, unless they are in an established job and over 40, may also have difficulty obtaining loans.[1]

There are two important points to be underlined in this quotation. Firstly, there are at present, 450 building societies and while they may belong to the Building Societies' Association, nevertheless they have their own rules and differ quite considerably in the way they operate. While one society may refuse a mortgage to a single person (and there *are* one or two which will not countenance single applicants) others would consider making a loan. The important thing is to try several societies and not to give up at a first refusal. Here the journalist quite rightly warns us that *some* societies might make it difficult for a single woman under forty and not in an established job to borrow but not all would insist on that ripe age. In fact I was advised to get a mortgage before I reached thirty-five in order to ensure that repayments could be made over twenty-five years. The later the mortgage loan is left, the heavier the monthly repayments must be. The number of single women who do in fact have mortgages proves that not all societies are wholly unwilling to make such loans.

Where loans are refused, it is usually because the society feels

[1] *Housebuyer*, January 1973, p. 21.

it would be almost impossible for the applicant to keep up the repayments and generally make ends meet, and so it would be unkind to allow him or her to embark upon the project.

Normally speaking, you should not expect a mortgage advance of more than two and a half times your annual income. Your chances of getting three times your salary are slim but should not be ruled out entirely. Whatever the amount advanced, the society may not allow your monthly repayments to exceed a quarter of your monthly earnings. If you borrow 90 per cent of the price of your home, you will still have to find 10 per cent to put down as a cash deposit.

When I made inquiries into the present situation regarding mortgage loans, I was assured that there was no discrimination either against single men or single women, but that obviously a building society must protect its own interests—that is the interests of its investors—for profit is not the aim of a building society which is a 'service' organisation, not a profit-making concern. Most of them are responsible enough to want to protect applicants too from taking on a burden that could be intolerable. It is far worse to have a mortgage and then find it impossible to keep up the repayments than never to have had a mortgage at all. For this reason a society would want to know that a regular salary was assured—hence the so called 'secure positions' that are recognised.

One step that is enormously helpful both in preparing to put down a deposit, and also in proving one's reliability to a society when applying for a loan, is to have a Savings Share account with them. Whether it is with the intention of saving for a deposit or for anything else, it is an excellent thing to save with a building society. The interest is good and it is one of the safest forms of investment. If you need the money at any time, it is perfectly easy to withdraw the capital. Clearly if you have saved with a society and it can be seen that one is disciplined in putting aside ten or twenty pounds on a regular basis, then one is in a far more favourable position when asking for consent to borrow money for a home.

The single people who really do find it difficult to obtain mortgages are those with irregular incomes. It is not primarily the amount of the salary that is taken into consideration but its regularity.

Even recognising that the position for single people may have additional problems to those faced by married couples, it is still worth pursuing the goal of a home of one's own. The goal may seem a very long way off but it would be sensible to keep it in view and start saving.

FURNISHING

Let us suppose then that a place has been found. How is it to be furnished and decorated? There may be precious little money left over after the house has been bought (and the deposit put down), legal fees paid, etc.

Does it all sound rather nerve-racking? It need not be! For many people the *real* fun starts, however, when the property has been bought. All the visits to the solicitor's office are over, the correspondence with the building society is completed for the time being, the contracts have been exchanged (or at least a date has been fixed for their exchange). Now comes the time for measuring up for curtains and carpets, the budgeting for furniture. This goes, too, for people who are moving into a flat or house that goes with their job. Some pieces may be acquired from the parental home, but the rest . . . ? Most of us, at this stage, have had our first experience of auction sales and perhaps second-hand shops. It has given us a tremendous kick to pick up a real bargain or to find an unexpected treasure.

Furnishing is nothing like as daunting as it may appear at first. There are plenty of 'do it yourself' ideas in magazines. They repay careful reading for they are often full of worthwhile hints on how to furnish on a shoestring. There are exciting ideas about fabrics and how to match up colours or set them off one against the other.

You may even feel challenged to do a bit of carpentry as well as needlework. I remember needing bookshelves and sawing

up an old wardrobe to make them. My desk at that stage was
also a home-made affair out of VIP board—but it served very
well. The desk lamp was made out of a footlight from the dis-
used stage at our church. Carpets were a major item and seemed
likely to be the most expensive. By a bit of searching around,
however, I discovered that there were ex-Admiralty (Wilton!)
carpets being sold off at a very reasonable price. My lounge is
still carpeted with one of them! You usually have to search for
bargains, but this can be fun.

I used to think it would be marvellous to have enough
money to be able to plan out one's entire home—decor,
furniture, fabrics, kitchen equipment, the lot . . . and have
everything absolutely new and to one's own individual taste.
Now I think the greater fun comes from 'making do' and
gradually building up the home you want—possibly still
clinging on to some of those bargain bits of furniture! Even
though the colours and shapes might not be just what you would
have had, given a completely free choice and unlimited
financial resources, there is still a good deal of choice and
personal taste in what you buy second-hand. The personality
still comes through, and the choosing, painting, renovating and
upholstering often provide greater outlets for the creative
instinct than the buying up of ready-made furniture and curtains would.

In the choosing of the decor, be daring, be ambitious, be
conventional, or whatever—but let it be *you*! As in dress so in
the home, try and let the outward appearance approximate as
nearly as possible to the inner you. Let the home be an expression and extension of your personality. As an expression of *you*
it will be truly satisfying (for it is not so much in the *possessing*
of a home that satisfaction comes but rather the opportunity it
gives to express oneself.)

Perhaps a special word of comfort is needed here. Those with
very limited financial and material resources, and this would
certainly apply to many missionaries, should be encouraged by
the example of Betsie Ten Boom and her transformed prison

cell. It is possible to find creative outlets and real fulfilment with very little in the way of material or human wealth. Self-expression is not entirely dependent upon financial security. Far more it stems from deep inner resources and imaginative resourcefulness.

At present many Societies cannot offer any permanent security to their missionaries. Sometimes they are unable even to offer sufficient pay to meet present material needs let alone future ones. Many missionaries have to forego the very securities which we have been considering in this chapter but nevertheless it is still possible for the basic home-making instinct to function and flourish. This would be perfectly evident if we were privileged to do a rapid tour of many mission stations. We should then be able to see how although God so often ministers to us through people and things, He can and does satisfy in the midst of real deprivation. Missionaries are by no means the only ones or even the worst off in this category. The same could be said of other homes of people who exist in real poverty. There must be countless heroic examples of those who have tried to bring a touch of beauty and homeliness into places of ugliness and squalor—their one slum room in a tenement block, their shanty town shack, their 'bit' of a dormitory in a refugee camp.

In this respect single people may have fewer difficulties than married couples. In marriage two sets of ideas, two different kinds of taste have got to be accommodated. It may so happen that they dovetail perfectly. It may be that one partner will dominate the other in the choices. More often than not there is a good deal of giving and taking to be done. It is not surprising that some of my married friends have told me that it has sometimes taken quite a while before they were won over to their partner's tastes. At least the single person need not consult anyone else before choosing. In this respect he can please himself.

On the other hand, on the question of household goods, the single person may be at a disadvantage compared with his married friends. A married couple usually start life in a new home with a shower of presents from relations and friends. Even if the bigger items of furniture are not given, kitchen equipment, china, cutlery and linen are often among the wedding presents. It is a very good start, for they have in one fell swoop what single people sometimes have to acquire over years. I wish we could emulate the American idea of a 'Shower' and arrange a party for our single friends who are just setting up house, with each guest bringing a present for the home. I feel sure people would be very happy to encourage single folk to start a home of their own in this way. It just needs a few people to help the idea 'catch on' and become part of our English way of life.

During the years when you are in digs or in a flat that goes with your job, or in rented accommodation, it is a good idea to start a collection of 'things for the home'. Why not begin to put aside things that would be useful in the home that you hope to have one day—even if you cannot see when that will be—rather than spend unnecessarily on cosmetics and clothes? It gives the same kind of satisfaction of building for the future as saving in a building society does.

Items of linen will always be useful so a collection of sheets and pillowslips, towels, tablecloths and tea towels will never be amiss.

Go ahead and collect sets of kitchen utensils, table mats, flower vases, candlesticks, cutlery, china and glass, trays, waste bins, lamps. Look forward with real anticipation to the day when you will have your own home. Friends may be glad to know that you are gathering things together like this because it will provide them with ideas for Christmas and birthday presents. If you start to build up a collection (I refrain from using the term 'bottom drawer' which seems to imply an expectation of marriage) it can be done slowly and with a great deal of thought and care. That is a great asset, for so often one has to live with one's choices for a very long time.

Buying up our equipment for the mission field was in some ways similar to preparing one's own home for married life. We felt particularly conscious that our choices were tremendously important, that away out in the bush we would need a certain elegance and daintiness. Tables could be rather rough and solid, but a dainty lace tablecloth would transform one. We would see enough of enamel mugs and plates, a really nice china tea set would give a great 'lift' on those days when one was feeling particularly homesick. Tropical colours are usually extremely vivid, so it can be restful to have delicate colours and subtle shades in the curtaining and bed covers.

When I reached the mission station to which I had been assigned, I realised very soon just how much graciousness mattered in isolated places. Cooking facilities might be reminiscent of a Guide camp but it didn't mean eating out of a billy can as though on perpetual safari. The world of the kitchen and the world of the dining room could be poles apart (as indeed they are in a lot of our restaurants in England).

A missionary colleague once invited a group of us to supper, and I remember feeling absolutely thrilled at the elegance of the meal. We had bathed and dressed for the occasion, and we were all out to enjoy an evening of leisure. Looking back I realise that the cuisine was not extraordinary. Food, in that area, was quite difficult to come by and we had a dish of peas and Spam in cheese sauce. I do not think I would find that particularly exotic now. But it wasn't the food that made the meal a sumptuous feast. It was the setting. She had a beautiful Scandinavian tablecloth. It was a rich, deep blue with exquisite silver embroidery around the edges, and in the centre. There were matching table napkins, also hand embroidered, while two lovely candles at each end of the table gave a soft and festive light. I still remember it all with deep pleasure. It was one of a number of occasions when a simple, very ordinary meal was enhanced by a setting that had imaginative touches of beauty and elegance.

What applied abroad applies really in any home-making.

Take trouble to find one or two elegant things that will bring you continual pleasure. It is so worthwhile having a few really beautiful things—and they don't necessarily have to be all that costly. A beautiful piece of stone or wood may be picked up on the beach for nothing but the colour and shape could be a source of constant delight.

One of the biggest temptations of living alone is that of not bothering too much about the manner in which you have meals. Best china may be put away and only used for visitors. It is easy to slip into the habit of grabbing a snack in the kitchen, not even taking time to sit down, when life is busy and there are pressures of work. If single people are so tempted, they would do well to read Edith Schaeffer's book, *Hidden Art*.[1] They would probably end up, as a friend of mine did, with at least a simple floral arrangement on their lunch tray. A lovely candle can transform a table, and is so much softer a light than the lamp. A piece of beautiful glass, a flower or an arrangement of shells make a refreshing centre-piece.

Gracious living requires imagination, not necessarily money. We can all have it; indeed we all need it. In a world that has much that is harsh and ugly in it, we should endeavour in these simple little ways to counteract that aspect. '. . . whatsoever things are lovely, think (and look) on these things' for they will soften, mellow, and add graciousness to our personalities.

Just before I finished my missionary training our Principal said to me; 'Margaret, when you get to Congo, whatever you do, *don't slum it*!' I wonder what there was about my life-style in college that prompted her to say that! Her words have come back to me often in my home in this country as well as abroad. To other single people who, like me, are not *primarily* interested in the domestic aspects of running a home, I pass them on as words of sound practical wisdom . . . yet more than that! It is wisdom based on biblical principles. The Bible teaches us that we are made in the image of God—and He is a God who loves and

[1] Edith Schaeffer, *Hidden Art* (Norfolk Press).

creates beauty. We have in us then not only a capacity to create but also to beautify. The marvel of it is, that you do not have to be a Norman Hartnell or a Josiah Wedgwood to do this. It is by simple, homely touches of beauty, within reach of us all, that we reflect the image of our Creator.

Put a great deal of imagination, thought and care into your home and you will then get a great deal out of it. You will have much to enjoy in it (so that you won't need or want to go out all the time), but also there will be much to share with others. Do use your home and accept it as a great gift. Many single people are not fortunate enough to have one. Build it up, make it beautiful and then *open* it. You will never be lonely if your home is the sort of place that others delight to share.

'Be given to hospitality' and give it very gladly.

There are times when one needs to be alone but it is easy to let this need become a selfish form of withdrawal. Homes are for loving and if we are so houseproud that we cannot open them to others, then we are indulging in a wrongful love of beauty and order. The home is one of those proper channels of loving that is open to single people. For them there is a greater freedom to help and care for others. Quite often they have more space than a family. It will not mean a major upheaval to a husband and all the children to bring home a distraught widow or an exhausted runaway.

Some friends of mine passed a lady who was sprawled across the seat in a bus shelter. She was making queer noises which they took to be drunken snores. There was something about the woman that made one of them hesitate however. Eventually they called an ambulance and the stranger was taken to hospital where it turned out she had suffered a slight stroke. They visited her in hospital and discovered that she was living alone in rooms near to their own flat. She had not a single, living relative. When she came out of hospital, they took her to their flat whilst she convalesced. They looked after her when she went back to her own rooms. They invited her to lunch every Sunday and continued to care for her very lovingly—a stranger they had met at a bus stop.

She was only one of many people they had helped in a similar way. The story of their flat would make a book in itself, yet because they opened it so freely and generously, they are amongst the most fulfilled single women I know.

Their willingness to help anyone who came to them in trouble points up another important factor. We cannot always be selective in our loving and this applies to the use of our homes. Such selectiveness could also amount to selfishness. I learned this in a curious way.

One extremely cold winter's afternoon, I lit a roaring fire in my lovely Cornish-stone fireplace, drew up the settee, plumped up the cushions, put my feet up and settled back for a cosy afternoon with a box of chocolates and a novel, with Polycarp (my cat) wrapped round my feet. The novel was *The Dean's Watch* by Elizabeth Goudge. I read of Mary Montague who was crippled by a fall as a child. In her dreams she planned a life full of adventures but gradually as she grew up, she realised that never would she embark on those adventures, and her chances of marriage were almost non-existent.

With no prospects of a career or marriage it seemed that she was doomed to life-long boredom. But then in a moment of awakening, it dawned upon her that *loving* could be a vocation in itself, a life work. It could be a career, like marriage, or nursing, or going on stage. Loving could be an adventure. Quietly, she accepted the vocation and took a vow to love.

God spoke to me through Mary Montague that afternoon, in the pages of Elizabeth Goudge's novel. For me it was also a moment of awakening. I suddenly saw how my loving had been lacking in energy because I had been harbouring resentment (against God, I suppose) that I hadn't a husband and children. Suddenly, what seems so obvious now, and what I had known and accepted in theory, came to me with new reality—not in prayer on my knees, but curled up on a settee with a box of chocolates and a novel. Loving could be a vocation in itself, loving on a wider scale than that of a family, loving in a kind of reckless outpouring that is not worried as to whether or not it will be loved in return.

I read on.

Mary Montague grew to love, dearer than all the rest, her brother Clive. It was he who had pushed her down the tower stairs as a child (thus crippling her for life). She patterned her love on the central figure of the Gospels. The love of Christ as she grew to discern him held and illumined every human being she met.

There come to us in life sudden moments of clarity, and this was one such moment for me. In the depths of my heart, where no words are needed, I knew that God was placing upon me a vocation for life, a vocation that would continue however much the outward pattern of my life might change.

Staring at the fire, I prayed to be delivered from the bondage of my own yearnings and longings and to be gloriously freed from the feverish desires that could block the path of such a vocation. Almost at once it seemed as though God showed me how I could make a start, by sharing my home with someone in need.

I put the novel on one side, and the chocolates. I left the fireside and abandoned—rather sadly at first—the prospect of a weekend of blissful solitude, and went to fetch a young colleague who lived in a very dingy bed-sit. I found her huddled over the one bar of a totally inadequate electric fire, still wearing the anorak that she had put on that morning whilst the room 'warmed up'. She came home with me and together we toasted our toes in front of the fire and talked into the night. For both of us there was far more warmth in that weekend than came from the fire blazing in the hearth.

For me, it was a turning point. It was the first conscious step
on a new path of obedience. I began to see exciting possibilities
if one worked at loving, as people have to work at their marriage if it is to grow and deepen, and God had shown me a
practical, down to earth starting point, an open heart and an
open hearth.

2. HOLIDAY-MAKING

The question of a holiday arises annually so, for single people,
there is the added decision to make 'With whom shall I go on
holiday this year?' Married people (or at least those who are
able to afford a holiday for themselves and their children) will
for the most part assume that they go away together. There are
the exceptional cases where married people are forced to take a
holiday separately, or not get a holiday at all—in order to keep
a business going or for other practical reasons. And there are a
few (only a very few I should imagine) who because of their
differing tastes, actually prefer to go their separate ways, the
husband going north to fish while the wife goes south to sun
herself on some beach. Generally, the question of company on
holiday does not arise for the married couple. They will go away
as a pair even if it is within a larger party.

For the single person there are a number of possibilities. He
can go alone, or with a friend, or in a small group, or with an
organised party (all of whom might be strangers to each other
at first) or with his parents. In that he usually does not have the
family commitments and expenses of a married man, he can
often contemplate holidays in exciting, faraway places—and, in
my opinion, should do more than contemplate them. There are
particular joys to be had within marriage and no one would be
ashamed to accept them and enjoy them. There are also particular joys within the single life. There is no need to be apologetic
about this. It is a way of meeting different people, seeing new
places and observing different customs. It is all part of a

broadening process which makes for maturity and gives experience which can be shared and enjoyed by others.

Not all, of course, want the bother of a lot of travelling, nor are all good travellers. Far more important than the distance covered is the question of whether or not this is going to be a truly refreshing and recreative experience. It may be a week in a little cottage only a few miles away from home, but if it helps to fulfil the holiday-maker by giving time for thought, sleep, doing nothing, getting exercise, enjoying new smells, new sights, different kinds of conversation, then it is immensely worth-while.

This may point to the importance in the choice of a holiday companion. People vary so much in their tastes. Some like to be really lazy and spend every day and all day just on a beach (maybe taking an occasional dip). Others get bored with such inactivity and want to be on the move, sightseeing, walking, sampling all sorts of foods, looking for the perfect subject for a photo. Sometimes married people can find it a problem to reconcile their differing needs on holiday!

Very often single people will go away with a close friend and this can make for an ideal and happy holiday. For even after the holiday is over, they can go on sharing reminiscences, viewing each other's slides and generally expanding their pleasure. But however friendly two people are, however well they may work together or enjoy everyday pursuits, if their ideas as to how best to spend a holiday differ very widely, it is far better for them to settle for separate holidays. A fortnight or more of close proximity with someone, continually disagreeing over how to spend precious holiday time (for which you are paying quite lavishly), could end in the kind of row that might end the friendship. We tend to put great expectations upon our holidays, hence the bitter disappointments if weather is quite awful, or the hotel is incomplete or even non-existent, or if one is taken ill. It can be equally disappointing if personal relationships on holiday prove a strain so that far from being rested and refreshed, you arrive back emotionally exhausted. Having given that word of caution about a careful choice of companion, let it be added that most friends who go away together do have a wonderful time and begin, almost at once, to plan their next year's holiday!

In these days there are so many organisations that arrange party holidays, no pair of friends need necessarily be entirely dependent upon each other's company. They can go away together yet within a much larger group which means that they can move around separately as well as together. If, too, they prefer to let someone else shoulder the responsibility of the travel and excursion arrangements, a party is an excellent idea. You can meet up with other people quite naturally without having to go through the traumatic ice-breaking that sometimes happens in hotels. Our British reserve makes us a little uncertain as to whether or not conversation will be welcomed or resented by other guests!

Holiday parties may also be the answer to a single person who is unable to fix a holiday with a friend. A single person on holiday alone does not necessarily imply that he is someone without a friend. Often it is difficult for two people to get holiday leave at the same time, especially if they work in the same office or ward. It is encouraging to discover that quite a lot of single people do take this way of holidaying nowadays, and mostly make friends very quickly.

During a recent cruise, I was amazed to discover how many people had come on holiday alone—both men and women, single, widowed and divorced. Within the first day, they had all paired up or joined a group and no one seemed 'left out'. On our table alone, there were three women all of whom had come on holiday by themselves. They met during the first evening aboard and from then on kept company throughout the cruise.

One of the advantages of such a holiday (and often they are no more expensive than staying at a hotel) is that you do have the opportunity to meet and get to know people (you can scarcely help it unless the liner is huge)—at meals, around the swimming pool, during entertainments or just talking generally in the lounge. Even going ashore, while there is complete freedom to roam around alone if you want to, you may keep together as a party and avail yourself of guides and transport provided. For the period of the cruise you are a floating community and the life is more of a shared life than is normal in hotels. Yet you can have as much privacy as you want with your own cabin and plenty of quiet places on deck.

GOING AWAY ALONE

While it is possible for people to go away on their own and be absorbed into a party such as you find on package tours or cruises, there are real problems for single people, especially women, who go alone to a hotel for a holiday. Even there they may meet with someone who is glad to have company, but for the most part the lone holiday-maker is a source of curiosity, concern, embarrassment — maybe all three — to others in the hotel. One journalist,[1] speaking of the single girl on holiday, has said:

She is a familiar figure in many people's holidays, the solitary woman at the table in the corner. Almost involuntarily, from the deep security of one's table laid for two, one stares and wonders what she's doing there, until one feels ashamed of such a show of curiosity. For goodness' sake, a single woman needs a holiday as much as you.

Although the lone holiday-maker may be tucked away at an obscure table by herself, she is still somehow conspicuous, and I judge that most women in this position *feel* conspicuous. In travelling around, I have sometimes had to stay in hotels on my own, and the part I most dread is walking into the dining room alone and facing the undisguised curiosity in people's stares. I always take a book with me so that I can become absorbed in it and don't have to spend the mealtime avoiding

[1] Fiona MacCarthy, *Evening Standard*, July 14th, 1971.

glances from other tables. I became so self-conscious at this kind of staring when staying in a hotel in Toronto that I was sorely tempted to round up the one or two other women on their own in the vast dining room and ask if we could not join forces. However a stubborn streak in me made me brazen it out. From such experiences I know that I would not choose a fortnight of that kind of embarrassment for a holiday, but others may feel far less sensitive about it and thoroughly enjoy not having to be sociable and make conversation.

A further, much more serious, difficulty these days is the near impossibility of booking a single room. If such rooms exist, the privilege of privacy costs extra. It may make economic sense to the hoteliers and to organisers of package tours, but it does seem horribly unfair to single people! As one woman said to me once: 'A holiday is the time when you most need your own room.' If one is used to sleeping alone, it can take quite a time to get used to the deep breathing of someone else in the room even if that someone else is your best friend. Disturbed sleep can make one feel extremely edgy and spoil part of the holiday. If one is used to living alone, it can be something of a strain suddenly to have to be in the company of another all the time. And as for having to share with complete strangers . . . well there comes a time when you will not only hate sharing rooms with strangers, but will make a single room a condition of a holiday.

This is one of the hazards married couples do not have to face when they go away. I wonder if they realise how strongly many single people feel about being allowed the same degree of privacy that they themselves are guaranteed. Why ever should one suffer for not being half a pair? And why should one have to pay extra each time one goes on holiday simply because one happens to be single? Perhaps it seems a small matter, but in discussion with single people, it is a point which recurs again and again—and not only with those who admit to being shy. Of course there are circumstances where one accepts that single rooms are impossible and one would not wish to embarrass or inconvenience anybody. An example that occurs to me is that of Oberammergau during the year of the Passion Play. I should think that every spare room and every spare bed is taken up night after night with the steady stream of visitors coming and going. It is such a privilege to be there at all that you would not want to press for personal comforts or ask for preference. Then too in war-time we accepted the most extraordinary sleeping arrangements, but in such willingness we must not confuse the particular with the general.

Single men may come off rather better than women in this matter of holidaying alone. We are more used to seeing men on their own in hotels for many commercial travellers and company representatives are forced to do this regularly. I have never had cause to put this to the test but I am told that one problem single women face is that confrontations with the manager can be difficult. A hotel manager is likely to take the complaints of a man more seriously than those of a woman. Rightly or wrongly, some hotel managers think they can 'fob off' a woman; but perhaps women are as much to blame in this as the hotel managers!

One further risk attached to this kind of holiday is that some men assume that a woman on her own is looking for a man. Perhaps she is. Some are quite open about the fact that they prefer to go on holiday alone, rather than with another woman, because men will befriend someone on her own whereas two women together are a daunting prospect. Such women go on holiday in search of companionship, and every blessing on them. There is no disgrace in that. Other women, however, find the attentions of men a nuisance and most unwelcome. Quite the biggest annoyance for women travelling around alone is the idea some men have that solitariness indicates availability. Sometimes a poor woman who has gone away to enjoy fresh sea breezes, music, walks and general exploration of the neighbourhood is forced to spend precious time as a virtual prisoner in her room in an attempt to dodge a man who is pressing his unwelcome attentions upon her. It is problems of this nature that make it more difficult for a woman to go out on her own at night to places of entertainment or even just for a stroll. This is more so in some countries abroad than here in the British Isles.

It can be doubly lonely for a solitary woman to be by herself on holiday in that erratic dream world which civilised men have concocted for themselves—an illusory society intent on endless jollity. A world built on curious mathematical principles where everybody has neatly to form themselves in pairs.[1]

In spite of all the problems that beset the woman holidaying alone, however, many still do it and actually enjoy it. They need holidays like anyone else in order to recharge the batteries. So, let them enjoy their holidays!

The people who deserve the greatest sympathy are those single people who never even try to get away for a holiday; who never see new places or meet new people. These miss a great deal. It may be lack of confidence that prevents them going away, or lack of money, or dependent parents, or ill health or just general lack of interest in anything beyond the home circle.

WITH PARENTS

The last word must be on the subject of holidays with parents. Family holidays can be a great joy and many single people with parents still alive would want *at times* to go away with one or other or both of their parents. Where such holidays begin to lose their enjoyment is when it is assumed that this will always be a pattern as unchanging as the law of the Medes and Persians. If the single person is never free to choose to get away with a friend or contemporaries on the kind of holiday older people would perhaps not enjoy or be able to cope with,

[1] Fiona MacCarthy, *Evening Standard*, July 14th, 1971.

then the family holiday can be a source of irritation. The bachelor or single girl may look very wistfully at brochures and hear others discussing their plans to do all sorts of exciting things and know that yet again, for the umpteenth year running, they are going to have to take 'Mum' to the same little guest house at Muddyplace-by-the-Wash and do exactly the same things as last year, *and* the year before and as far back as they can remember. They will grind on in the same rut for another year. Single people should not be *expected* to go away every year with their ageing parents, nor is it wise for them to do so.

This is true especially of those who live with parents all the year round. A complete break and holiday with contemporaries is almost essential. It can of course be very difficult to arrange to be away if Mother and/or Father is frail and cannot be left alone. Yet arrangements can be made for this even if it means a friend or relative coming in to stay during the son or daughter's absence. Or possibly it will mean that Mother or Father will have to go to a nursing home for two weeks (this only in extreme cases when nursing is needed and there is no other member of the family willing to help out). So often the single person who is left living at home, caring for elderly parents all the year round, is also expected by them and by other members of the family to shoulder the responsibility of taking them away on holiday, or going without a holiday altogether.

It is not uncommon for an elderly parent to resist very strongly the son or daughter going away, even for a short holiday. The very thought fills them with dread and they put up all sorts of barriers, excuses, reasons. There may be painful scenes and 'Mother' may have 'one of her turns'. This is the commonest of all defence mechanisms. It is not that illness is feigned. It is simply an unconscious way of making the point that 'I simply cannot be left'. We may roar with laughter at the scheming, crafty devices of Steptoe to keep Harold tied to his apron strings. It may be amusing to see that pained and martyred expression and hear his trembling voice declare:

14

'I'm just a poo-or, old man . . . ' whenever he cannot get his
own way, but it is no joke when this happens in real life. The
son or daughter may wriggle and squirm to break loose just for a
short while, but they cannot do it for they are gripped as though
in an emotional vice.

If this is the predicament of a single person, then he needs an
ally. He needs someone to help him distinguish between the
genuine heart attack or 'turn' and one that is brought on by a
seeming opposition to the parent's will. It would be wise to
consult the doctor and get his advice and help. He may suggest
that a nursing home is a 'must' if the old person is going to
express his/her distress and displeasure by becoming ill. It
may need a third party such as a minister, doctor or friend to
tell 'Mother' or 'Father' that he/she is being selfish and
behaving rather childishly. An outsider of this standing could
help a great deal by pointing out how much the son or daughter
does all the year round and how a break is essential if he/she is
to keep well enough through the winter to look after them (the
parents).

It may well come to the point where some straight talking of
this kind has to be done, but it is never easy. It is important
that old people should be helped to remain adult as long as
possible. Once we start giving in to their tantrums and childish
whims, once we get to the stage where none dare cross them or
differ from them in any way, we are hastening their second
childhood and resigning ourselves to their inevitable and steady
decline. The only appropriate course of action then is to
humour and tolerate the 'child'. Few of us like spoiled children
or find them attractive; similarly, few of us really like spoiled
'elderly children' who only have to be difficult to get their own
way.

Hard as it may be then, single people really need to be quite
firm with parents in this matter of holidays. If they are adult
and financially independent, then they must not allow themselves to be overruled year after year. Perhaps this sounds
harsh, but it is not intended to be. Of course it is always simpler

to suggest a right way of going about things than to follow it. For some the position is very difficult indeed—and you cannot really judge how difficult it is unless you have had to face it personally. It may be possible for those with sufficiently long holidays to take the parents away for a short holiday regularly while at the same time retaining their own holidays, outlets, friends and so forth.

The important thing in this whole matter is to see that all parties behave and are treated as fully adult, and that holidays together are not a burden but a delight.

3. HANDLING FINANCES
(For women only)

Many single women are highly competent in financial matters and handle all their affairs most efficiently. They are the equal of any man in this respect, and, indeed, it is not uncommon to find married women coping with the finances even within a marriage.

There are, however, quite a large number of single women who really feel most inadequate when it comes to facts and figures. Income-tax-return forms are a nightmare and they do not even understand their salary statements. A number of my friends have confessed to incompetence in these sort of matters, and yet they are intelligent, responsible people. I used to think that if ever I married that would be the part of my life that I would hand over most thankfully to my husband—the paying of the bills and the mortgage repayments, the claims on and payments of insurance, the taxing of the car and the drawing of National Health benefit. They all require forms and documents and policy numbers which I find confusing and worrying! But while these responsibilities are present realities, we cannot just be ostriches. They must be faced and dealt with satisfactorily.

First of all then, the admission that many single women cope very uneasily with their finances may be an encouragement to those who thought they were alone in their deficiencies, to those who assumed that all their other single friends managed smoothly and efficiently, never finding this area of life a burden. Be assured, if you have problems, you are one of many!

Secondly, has it occurred to you to have a financial director? Many of us are glad enough to have a spiritual director who will guide and advise on spiritual matters. Why should we be ashamed to admit the need of someone to help us with our temporal affairs? I think we are so anxious not to give the impression of the 'helpless little woman' that we tend to go to the other extreme of attempting to brave it out with a show of false competence. If among our men friends, there is someone we can trust utterly, who is good with accounts and figures, why not sink a little pride and enlist his help? Sometimes it is a help even to discuss such things as income-tax returns and ask for difficult terms to be explained. It is certainly a good thing to have the support and advice of someone 'who knows about these things' when it comes to larger matters such as buying a car or a house. In the matter of a house, of course, there will be proper legal advice and not much likelihood of a swindle, but in the matter of cars, sadly it is usually inadvisable for a woman to try and negotiate a price on her own. It is a good policy to take a man along to look over the car, test it out and haggle about the price, for many women are hopelessly out of their depth in this realm. Some of the more practically minded women who understand mechanics and know a good deal about current prices on the car market may by now be livid at reading the above advice. If you are in that category, I can only assure you that you are a minority group within our sex!

All walks of life bring their responsibilities as well as their privileges, and while we may enlist the help of a 'financial director', we cannot opt out of *all* our responsibilities in this field. Some women are ultra-efficient about paying bills while others are negligent. We can arrange for the bank to pay our regular bills but others we can only deal with ourselves. Single women who are working to their limit in their professional spheres are among the worst offenders in this respect. It is not that they *intend* to be defaulters, or even inconvenience others. It is rather that bills are pushed to one side on the desk to be dealt with in a spare moment and perhaps there are no such moments for quite a while. Other things get piled on top of the bills and are forgotten till perhaps a demand note jogs the memory. In a discussion among professional, single women, several pleaded guilty to this particular 'crime' of negligence and vowed to go back and clear their desks of all outstanding bills.

It is also wise to keep careful records of all additional earnings. If a friend is to advise you, he will need to know all the facts. In a career where there are extra fees paid for lecturing, broadcasting, writing, leading courses at conferences, reading manuscripts, helping in an advisory capacity, or if there are ways in which extra money is coming in through practical help such as dressmaking, cake icing, decorating, car maintenance, hairdressing, it is important to make a comprehensive list of extra earnings and to keep the dates, receipts, invoices and any other relevant information. It is so easy to think the odd pound or two is unimportant, but negligence here can lead to later difficulties with the Inland Revenue.

Often a single woman (or man) has to finance a home on a single salary whereas a married couple may have just the same mortgage repayments, almost the same electricity and gas bills to pay, and yet have a double salary coming in to help meet those expenses. It is a help to have the advice of a financial director as to how best to economise. There are a number of hints that friends can give as to how to curb expenditure if finances are a bit tight. If it should be that there is money and enough to spare, it may be good to get advice as to how best to save or invest it.

I do feel that all too often single women try to 'go it alone',

carrying quite heavy financial burdens. Some get into difficulties while others do not get the maximum benefit from their
money. Some are not getting paid the proper salary, yet do not
know how to set about righting the situation. A man is often
far less embarrassed about asking questions, probing and sifting
facts, than women are. Yet it is not a responsible attitude to let
things slide or live in a kind of financial euphoria. If we are
prepared to help each other as friends and 'bear one another's
burdens', then this too must be shared. Surely within the Body
of Christ at any rate we should not be ashamed to admit to our
weaknesses as well as our strengths. Maybe in a local church
there is a man in banking or insurance or other professions
dealing with finance, who would willingly make his services and
advice available to church members. This has already been
tried in some church communities and has been of enormous
help to those 'in the family' who have problems in handling
financial matters.

Help in this direction will ultimately lead to more efficiency,
which will in turn redound to the greater glory of God. If we
are seen to be reliable in matters of money, people will find it
easier to trust us in other things.

CHAPTER ELEVEN

Single Blessedness

I HAVE DISCUSSED MANY OF THE PROBLEMS WHICH THOSE 'WHO walk alone' face, but in conclusion to this consideration of the single life I want to emphasise the joys and blessings as well. For joys there most certainly are, and blessings too—to the single people themselves and, please God, to those with whom they come into contact. Fulfilment and marriage are not to be treated as equal to each other. Some people will undoubtedly be fulfilled in marriage, but others find fulfilment in singleness.

Fulfilment has to do with filling full—that is, enjoying life to the full so that it is filled with a sense of purpose and meaning, with adventure and service. If our lives are 'hid with Christ in God', then we can accept that, whether we walk alone or in partnership, it is our vocation. And the only thing to do with a vocation is to accept it and follow it gladly. Why waste good energy chafing against it? If it changes later from a vocation to singleness into a vocation to marriage, then it will be a better start to the new life if one has learned acceptance of the old. The mind will have formed habit tracks of contentment that will carry over and will sweeten the path ahead.

They were such wise words of St. Paul when he said: 'I have learned in whatsoever state I am therewith to be content . . . I know both how to be abased and how to abound.'[1] It is rather

[1] Philippians 4: 12.

like a riverbed that may be a dried up muddy trickle at one moment and a raging torrent, sufficient to burst its banks, the next. Think how St. Paul might have enlarged upon his words, had he been invited to do so:

Questioner: 'Paul, do you really mean "in whatsoever state . . ."?'

Paul: 'Yes, I do. Acceptance is the key to positive living. I know how to be alone and how to be in company; how to be thrilled and how to be disappointed; how to be exhausted and how to be bursting with energy; how to put up with my troublesome 'thorn' and how to be painfree; how to be utterly serious and how to be hilarious; how to be sickened by my lust and how to rejoice in my sexuality; how to meet trouble and how to avoid it; how to be wounded by what people say and how to be encouraged by it; how to be used and how to be ignored . . .' and so it could go on.

A contented person is such a restful person! It is all too easy for single people to sigh for the green, green grass of their married friends' gardens and to fall prey to moments of panic when they see their future as sour old maids or crusty bachelors — embittered and frustrated by life's denials. There is absolutely no need for anyone to become sour, crusty, embittered or frustrated. For frustration does not necessarily stem from not having a spouse but comes from not having the opportunity to love. Frustration implies blocked up channels. Some channels of loving *are* blocked for single people, but there are plenty more that are open and through which their warm, deep love can flow with even greater force and energy. Did you never as children squirt water at one another, getting a tremendously forceful jet by blocking with a finger part of the outlet on the tap?

We need to distinguish here between frustration and limitation. There are those who say that they are *frustrated* when what they mean is that they are *limited*. There are, of course, limitations within the single life (and many of them have already been considered in previous chapters) but there must be quite as many in marriage. The girl with a good mind and an active brain, who did extremely well at school and university and was judged to be 'going places' could begin to feel frustrated (in the sense of limited) by a life that seems largely to revolve around the twin poles of the oven and the washing machine. For her the path of love means a denial of some (though let us hope not all) of her intellectual pursuits. The woman who has always been free to get out and about, to follow her own inclinations in the evenings, to pop up to town to the theatre or shops, or to make flying weekend visits to her numerous friends, is not always going to find it easy to adjust to the more settled life of marriage.

Every day a mother must make sacrifices of time and energy and practise considerable self-denial. Rather than think the grass of marriage is far greener than that of the single state, it might be more realistic to think in terms of exchanging one set of problems for another.[1]

An acceptance of one's limitations, contentment with one's calling, means that one is free to enjoy the present to the full. It seems a wrongful use of time always to be living in the future. It is an unhelpful use of the imagination constantly to build castles in the air. 'Live in the present reality and get the maximum enjoyment from it' seems a far more positive and worthwhile formula for happy, single life.

So, you are single—well rejoice in it! It does not mean that you have given up all hopes of marrying one day but it *does* mean that you will be a happier person than the one who is sorry for herself. Remember, happy people are attractive people and that in itself should increase the marriage prospects! But far more important than that is that happiness helps a person to live positively. Negativism is so gloomy, and wearing and enervating.

I know there are some who feel at this stage that they cannot

[1] *Viewpoint* No. 11 (S.U.), 'Is Marriage out of Date?'. p. 16.

face a life of walking alone. Some have said to me, 'I just cannot accept that I am always going to be single.' There are times when, of course, it is very hard as one sees the future yawning ahead like a lonely great chasm. But what is the alternative to not accepting life as it comes? Non-acceptance leads to bitterness and self-pity, both of which are most unattractive and ultimately destructive. To all single people who as yet find it difficult to rejoice in their singleness I would say: 'Do beware of the pit of self-pity. Once you have fallen into that, it is so hard to struggle out.' St. Paul really does seem to have found the antidote to the poison of self-pity when he says: 'In everything give thanks . . .' Don't wait to *feel* thankful, just give thanks anyway. Gradually this act of will is bound to change the attitude of mind and heart. As one writer has said, there are times when we have to learn to praise God 'through gritted teeth'.

THANKS—FOR FREEDOM!

Just think of all that there is for which we can give thanks. First and foremost, FREEDOM. We have already discussed some of the possible freedoms—such as having a home and all that that entails, freedom to travel, freedom to follow a career, freedom to develop and expand personal interests, freedom to widen one's circle of friends, freedom to choose between company and solitude, freedom to grow as an individual, freedom to give time, money and talents to whatever cause pulls at the heartstrings. The list could stretch on and on. Marjorie Holmes has expressed this extremely well in her prayer, The Lovely Solitude:[1]

I've just come from visiting a big noisy family and I'm exhausted. Filled with happy memories yes, but glad to get home.

And now seems a good time to realise that instead of

[1] From *Who Am I, God?* (Hodder and Stoughton).

lamenting my loneliness, I should be singing the blessings of solitude!

Thank you for silence, Lord. Sheer silence can indeed be golden. And so can order. I gaze about this apartment with new respect; it seems beautiful right now, and simple to keep it so with nobody to pick up after but myself.

And independence—how divine. The freedom to do what I please.

I can listen to the kind of music or watch the kind of television shows I really enjoy. I can read, write, sew, paint or just think without being interrupted.

I can read in bed at night as late as I want without disturbing anybody. I don't have to worry about anybody else's feelings, or have my own unexpectedly hurt. I don't have to argue or pretend to agree when I don't.

I don't have to be bored. I can give a party. I can call up a friend for lunch.

And even if all the people I know are busy, I have only to dial a few numbers, travel a few blocks to be in the thick of those who'll welcome me with open arms. My club, my church—hospitals, the Salvation Army.

More places than I can count, where there are always vital, joyous, stimulating people; and people whose loneliness and needs so far surpass mine that I feel richly endowed and aglow.

Lord, let me remember all this when loneliness gets me down.

And let me remember it also when I get too enamoured with solitude. Don't let me become ingrown and selfish.

There is so much work to be done and so many people to be helped and enjoyed. Especially for the woman who lives alone.

Apart from the freedom *for* certain joys, there is freedom *from* others such as family anxieties; freedom from the worry of the husband's prospects, the children's health, the disturbed nights with a crying baby, shortage of money and hungry little mouths to be fed; the inability to get away for a holiday break, a child unhappy at school, the daughter who has run away, the son in trouble with the police, the unwanted pregnancy, the threat of redundancy, the fear of unfaithfulness or divorce.

In fact, there can be so much freedom in the single life (I exclude those who are looking after elderly parents) that one has to guard against selfishness. We need always to remember that freedom is *for* greater service to others—not just for selfish indulgence. For true freedom implies a heart at leisure from itself.

The possibilities for exploring love within that freedom are endless and exciting. Moreover, the creative urge which is in all of us may still produce its offspring even though they be not of flesh and blood. History will demonstrate how often a particular establishment, movement, cause or monument has been 'conceived' and 'carried' by those who are single till, in time, they bring it forth as a gift to the world.

Gilbert Russell, in his book *Men and Women,* expresses what I have been saying:[1]

The three great ends of marriage hold good ... in the deepest sense, not only for husbands and wives but for single people as well. They also can be united, in affection and common life, with another or more than one. They can 'reproduce themselves' in a host of creative ways, in work and friendship and service to other folk. What they give to the world is often more precious than sons. The fabric of civilisation could not have been reared without them, and could hardly be maintained. Their gifts to mankind may endure beyond any posterity. Their 'society' gladdens and they bless with their 'help and comfort' uncounted men and women. We have all rejoiced in the friendship of people like this. 'Frustration' is a word which dies in their company.

[1] Op. cit., p. 77.

Bibliography

Allshorn, Florence, *Notebooks*, S.C.M.

Canadian Ecumenical Institute, *Report of a study of the Faith and Order Commission of the Canadian Council of Churches. The Biblical and Theological Understanding of Sexuality and Family Life*. November 1969

Caussade, J. P. de, *Self Abandonment and Divine Providence*, Burns, Oates & Washbourne 1959

Davidson, Alex, *Returns of Love*, I.V.P.

Dolling, R.R., *Ten Years in a Portsmouth Slum*, Brown, Longlan & Co. 1903

Edna Mary, Sister, *The Religious Life*, Penguin Books

Goudge, Elizabeth, *Green Dolphin Country*, *The Dean's Watch*, Hodder & Stoughton

Hillman, James, *In Search*, Hodder & Stoughton

Hodgson, Leonard, *The Doctrine of the Trinity*, Nisbett

Holmes, Marjorie, *I've Got to Talk to Somebody God*, *Who Am I God?* Hodder & Stoughton

Home, Evelyn, *Personal Problems Today*

Hutton, Laura, *The Single Woman: her Adjustment to Life and Love*, London, Barrie and Rockcliff

Lewis, C. S., *Letters to an American Lady*, Hodder & Stoughton, *The Four Loves*, Collins, Fontana

Marshall, Catherine, *To Live Again*, Peter Davies

Mehl, Roger, *Society and Love*, 'Société et Amour', Geneva 1961

Mitting, Elizabeth, *The Single Woman*, Victory Press

Moorhouse, Geoffrey, *Against All Reason*, Wiedenfeld & Nicolson

Novak, Michael, *The New Nuns*, Sheed & Ward

Padwick, Constance, *Temple Gairdner of Cairo*, S.P.C.K.

Pasquier, Jacques, *Celibacy and Affective Maturity*, from *The Way*, Journal of the English Jesuits

Pittenger, Norman, *Time for Consent*, S.C.M.

Quoist, Michel, *Prayers of Life*, Logos Books. Gill & Son

Royden, Maude, *A Threefold Cord*, Gollancz

Russell, Gilbert, *Men and Women*, S.C.M.

Schaeffer, Edith, *The Hidden Art*, Norfolk Press

Schaeffer, Francis, *The Mark of the Christian*, Hodder & Stoughton

Stephenson, Colin, *Merrily on High*, D.L.T.

Streeter & Appasamy, *The Sadhu*, MacMillan

Taizé, *The Rule*, Faith Press

Ten Boom, Corrie, *The Hiding Place*, Hodder & Stoughton

Thielicke, Helmut, *The Mystery of Sexuality*, Hodder & Stoughton

Thurian, Max, *Marriage and Celibacy*, S.C.M.

Vann, Gerald, *To Heaven with Diana*, Collins

Waugh, Evelyn, *Ronald Knox*, Chapman & Hall

Weatherhead, Leslie, *Psychology, Religion and Healing, Psychology in the Service of the Soul*, Hodder & Stoughton